SCHOOL LIBRARY MEDIA SERVICES TO THE HANDICAPPED

SCHOOL LIBRARY MEDIA SERVICES TO THE HANDICAPPED

Edited by Myra Macon

Greenwood Press
Westport, Connecticut • London, England

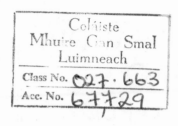
Library of Congress Cataloging in Publication Data
Main entry under title:

School library media services to the handicapped.

Bibliography: p.
Includes index.
Contents: A history of the education of the handi-
capped / by Austin W. Bunch--Federal legislation /
by Kieth C. Wright--Characteristics of the handi-
capped / by Kieth C. Wright--[etc.]
1. School libraries--Services to the handicapped--
United States.   2. Instructional materials centers--
Services to the handicapped--United States.   I. Macon,
Myra.
Z675.S3S29116   027.6′63   81-4262
ISBN 0-313-22684-9 (lib. bdg.)   AACR2

Library of Congress Catalog Card Number: 81-4262
ISBN: 0-313-22684-9

First published in 1982

Greenwood Press
A division of Congressional Information Service, Inc.
88 Post Road West
Westport, Connecticut 06881

Printed in the United States of America

10 9 8 7 6 5 4 3 2 1

CONTENTS

TABLE
AND
FIGURES

INTRODUCTION

The Education for All Handicapped Children Act (Public Law 94-142) which became effective in 1978 mandates that handicapped students with exceptional educational needs be educated in the least restrictive environment. The enactment of this law has added new dimensions to the roles of school library media specialists. Media specialists must take an active part in working with special education teachers and members of each Child Study Team to plan Individualized Educational Programs (IEPs), as well as work with regular classroom teachers in order to meet the individual needs of all children in the school.

The school library media center and the media specialist must provide resources to meet the basic informational needs of the handicapped student and are often required to obtain special format materials, special equipment and aids to help them cope with daily living, as well as educational expectations.

School Library Media Services to the Handicapped is intended to provide an overview of handicapped students who are mainstreamed into the school library media centers. While it is directed primarily at the school media specialist, attention has also been given to the need for a better understanding of the relationship of the school media specialist to the philosophy of special education programs and legislation, curriculum planning, and individualized programs for the handicapped students in public schools. This book introduces the reader to information on the history, characteristics, resources, IEPs, federal legislation and funding, and national library services for the handicapped. A selected annotated bibliography, a selected list of goals and activities for use with handicapped students, and an appendix listing companies, agencies, and institutions that supply materials and services to the handicapped complete the volume.

This book evolved from a two week workshop sponsored by the Graduate School of Library and Information Science at the University of Mississippi on services to the handicapped. The workshop was funded by the Department of Health, Education, and Welfare, Office of Education, Library Training Program, Title II-B Higher Education Act of 1965.

The following professionals served as consultants at the workshop and have also provided material for this book: Dr. Austin W. Bunch, Assistant Professor of Special Education, University of Mississippi; Dr. Barbara H. Baskin, Director of the Office of Special Education, SUNY, Stony Brook, New York; Ms. Ellen C. Fagan, Speech-Language Pathologist, Lexington County School District Five, Columbia, South Carolina and part-time Instructor in Communicative Disorders, University of South Carolina; Ms. Karen H. Harris, Associate Professor of Library Science, University of New Orleans, Louisiana; Ms. JoEllen Ostendorf, Head of Services for the Handicapped, Mississippi Library Commission, Jackson, Mississippi; Dr. Kieth C. Wright, Chairman of the Department of Library Science and Educational Technology, University of North Carolina at Greensboro.

ABBREVIATIONS

AAMD   American Association on Mental Deficiency
APH   American Printing House for the Blind
BEH   Bureau of Education for the Handicapped
BRS   Bibliographic Retrieval System
COH   Committee on the Handicapped
CST   Child Study Team
DB   Deaf-Blind
ED   Seriously Emotionally Disturbed
EH   Emotionally Handicapped
EMH   Educable Mentally Handicapped
EMR   Educable Mental Retardation
ERIC   Educational Resources Information Centers
HOH   Hard of Hearing
IEP   Individualized Educational Program
IIP   Individualized Instructional Plan
KRM   Kurzweil Reading Machine
LD   Specific Learning Disability
LEA   Local Education Agency
NLS   National Library Service for the Blind and Physically
           Handicapped
NTIS   National Technical Information Service

OH   Orthopedically Handicapped
OHI   Other Health Impaired
OI   Orthopedically Impaired
PARC   Pennsylvania Association for Retarded Children
PMH   Totally Dependent or Profoundly Mentally
          Handicapped
RFB   Recording for the Blind
RFP   Requests for Proposals
RFS   Requests for Services
SEA   State Education Agency
TMH   Trainable Mentally Handicapped
TMR   Trainable Mental Retardation
TSI   Telesensory Systems, Inc.
TSP   Total Service Plan
VH   Visually Handicapped

SCHOOL LIBRARY MEDIA
SERVICES TO
THE HANDICAPPED

1

A HISTORY OF
THE EDUCATION OF
THE HANDICAPPED

Austin W. Bunch

The formal education of handicapped children and youth is a relatively recent phenomenon. Although historical accounts of education for the handicapped differ, most agree that provisions for educational services did not begin until the late eighteenth century and did not experience substantial growth until the mid-twentieth century.

To place the impetus for educational programs in proper perspective, societal and governmental treatment of the handicapped prior to the advent of systematic attempts at education must be acknowledged. The treatment of the handicapped followed the pattern of predominate sociopolitical and religious beliefs of the major periods of history. Various authors have discussed the historical origins of education and treatment of the handicapped and have provided established eras that are generally commensurate with the major periods of recorded history. Such divisions of time and events lend a frame of reference to understanding the popular notions of regard for and treatment for individuals considered by their societies as "different."

Frank Hewett details the plight of the handicapped into four historical determiners: the need for survival, the force of superstition, the findings of science, and the desire to be of service. He acknowledges that within the time periods of these four determiners of treatment of the handicapped there are inconsistencies and incidences out of the synchrony. Such variations related to geography as well as isolated circumstances of changes in attitudes toward the handicapped. Overall, however, the chronology of events is rather stable and can be considered as indictive of the then popular beliefs about the way the handicapped should be treated. The treatment during the periods of history have been determined by philosophy, science, religion, and human nature.

The handicapped have been subjected to physical and mental torture, rejection, exploitation, as well as having been considered to reflect "divine" qualities. Their disabilities have been explained, rather crudely at times, in terms of levels of scientific knowledge and of superstitious belief. Current trends toward acceptance and inclusion in mainstream society represent tremendous humane strides that have evolved.

Early History

Bill Gearhart describes the earliest history of treatment of the handicapped as the "era of superstition." This era encompasses the period of time from the early Greek and Roman empires to the beginning of the creation of institutions in Europe and the United States in the eighteenth century. It was dominated by the beliefs that mentally retarded and other severely handicapped individuals were monsters and fools incapable of self-preservation. The early Greeks dealt with them severely; the treatment they received was accordingly inhuman. The handicapped were thrown off mountains, drowned in rivers, or simply left to the elements to die. Roman history includes references to exploitation of the handicapped through their use as court jesters and fools for personal amusement. All of the handicapped were not so lucky. Many were sentenced to death or were left to fend for themselves in the wilderness. This meant eventual death for most.

The Middle Ages found the handicapped again used as sources of ridicule and personal amusement. The nobility often kept handicapped individuals as court jesters or for personal sport. But it was during the Middle Ages that the growth of Christianity provided the feebleminded and physically handicapped with the opportunity for care and humane treatment. There are accounts that Christian morality was reflected in the consideration by some of the mentally and physically defective as beings sent from God. Their gibberish was considered "heavenly communication."

During this period care was provided for the handicapped by some European religious groups, particularly the Roman Catholic church. Gearhart notes that the most famous asylum for the mentally handicapped during this period was established by St. Vincent de Paul and his Sisters of Charity. Asylum was offered for sanctuary and safety from society rather than for educational purposes.

Asylum was also provided by individuals. Tycho Brahe, the renowned astronomer, reportedly kept a mentally retarded male companion for a "divine revelation." Brahe expected a voice from God to come through the mutterings and gibberish of his companion. There are other accounts of special treatment for the handicapped based on the notion that they were indeed gifts of God and, therefore, divine creatures.

Attempts to provide other than asylum were dealt with according to the philosophy of the times. A. E. Whitney gives an account of an attempt by a Spanish physician to educate retarded children in the early seventeenth century which resulted in the physician's expulsion from the country.

The Christian treatment of the handicapped was subsequently altered as a result of the changes in Christian doctrine following the Protestant Reformation. Both the mentally ill and the mentally retarded were viewed by Reformation leaders as demonic creatures. Evidence of Satanic qualities was shown through the convulsions and nonsense gibberish of the handicapped. Gearhart reports that Martin Luther and John Calvin regarded the handicapped as Godless creatures. Luther wrote that such individuals did not have a soul and that the void was filled by the Devil.

Hewett provides isolated accounts of educational opportunities for the blind in Egypt, Japan, and France. These instructional programs were for the purpose of producing scholars, musicians, and, in Japan, masseurs and acupuncture specialists. The Middle Ages provided a few notable attempts at education for the mentally and physically handicapped, but no systematic education. In general, religious beliefs, superstition, and fear dominated the treatment afforded the handicapped.

The Beginning of Special Education

The French Revolution and the changes that it brought in man's view of man provided a shift in the philosophy of society's responsibilities toward its less fortunate members. During the late eighteenth and early nineteenth centuries notable events in the treatment of the handicapped occurred. These included treatment of the mentally ill in an attempt to restore their reason by Pinel; a scientific approach to teaching deaf-mutes by Pereire which included the development of the lip-reading method; and the first scientific program of instruction for the mentally retarded by Dr. Jean Marc Gaspard Itard through his work with Victor, the wild boy of Aveyron.

Itard's ambitious and dedicated work with Victor, considered to be the beginning of special education, began with the accidental discovery by hunters of a "wild boy" of eleven or twelve years of age living in a forest in southern France around the turn of the nineteenth century. The naked youth's behavior suggested he led an animal-like existence. The boy was captured and sent to Paris for placement in the national institute for deaf-mutes where Dr. Itard served as chief medical officer. He observed the boy's behavior very closely. His impressions were that the boy was not incurable; that he, in fact, was only without formal training in civilized behavior. Itard asked for and received permission to become the child's guardian, convinced that through intense training the youth could become normal. Gearhart provides Itard's adopted aims for instruction with Victor as:

1. To interest him in social life
2. To awaken his nervous system
3. To extend the range of his thought
4. To lead him to the use of speech
5. To make him exercise simple mental operations to satisfy his physical needs.[1]

Itard worked with the boy he called Victor for a period of five years. His reports of this work were published in 1801 and 1806. In the first report, covering the first nine-month instructional program, Itard indicated that Victor had developed normal habits of sleeping, eating, and personal hygiene and that he had become sensorially aware of touch, taste, and smell. He also reported that Victor displayed an emotional dependence upon Itard's female housekeeper. Itard continued his instructional program for four more years. There were significant advances made in Victor's discrimination abilities—tactile, gustatory, auditory, and visual, but Victor remained essentially mute. Despite the significant gains made, Victor's failure to achieve normalcy prompted Itard to conclude that his experiment was a failure and that the boy was indeed mentally retarded and, therefore, incurable. The youth lived another twenty years under the care of Itard's housekeeper. He died at about age forty.

Itard's records of his work with Victor demonstrate the first thorough, clinical planning of an individualized program of study and instruction with an evaluation of the success or failure of the plan. This attempt is all the more noteworthy when it is considered that Itard was working with a severely handicapped individual. Thus, the foundation for modern-day special education was laid.

The major outcome of Itard's educational intervention was to stimulate interest in the education of the mentally retarded. Itard particularly influenced Edouard Seguin, his medical protégé. Seguin expanded the concepts of education for the handicapped provided by Itard into a physiological approach to education. The physiological approach emphasized the education of the whole child. His approach fostered the development of many teaching methods and materials still used in special and regular classrooms today, for example, pegboards, buttoning and lacing materials, and visual-training devices.

Seguin's educational program was very successful and attracted worldwide attention. He established the first school program specifically for the mentally retarded in Paris in 1837. His procedures for education and treatment were detailed in his classic textbook, *Idiocy and Its Treatment by the Physiological Method*. The book gained Seguin recognition and acclaim by the French Academy of Science.

The political climate in France changed abruptly with Napoleon's rise to power in 1848. Fear and unhappiness at the loss of personal freedom of thought led Seguin to leave France for the United States. He practiced medicine for a while in Ohio, and later became instrumental in establishing America's first residential facility for the retarded with education as its major focus. By his death in 1880 he had served a major role in the development of residential institutions for the retarded in several northeastern states. In 1876 he served as the first president of a newly formed organization of medical officers of institutions for the retarded. This organization evolved into the present-day American Association on Mental Deficiency (AAMD), one of the nation's most prestigious professional organizations.

Seguin's work and writings strongly influenced an Italian physician, Dr. Maria Montessori, the first woman in Italy to graduate in medicine from the University of Rome. Dr. Montessori was given the task of selecting and studying mentally retarded children in institutions. Her observations led her to believe that mental retardation was not as much a medical problem as an educational one. She adapted many of Seguin's methods and materials to educating the mentally retarded. By modern standards her work was very successful; the children she had worked with passed the examinations necessary to earn a primary education certificate. She felt that the methodology would be of greater use with normal children, and opened the first Montessori school, or "Children's House," in a poor section of Rome. The school was a success and allowed her to do what Seguin had dreamed of—merge regular education with special education.

Montessori's approach follows the natural physiological and psychological development of the child. Her program was divided into three major areas: motor education, sensory education, and language. The educational enforcement created by Montessori used child-sized tables, chairs, furniture, shelves, etc. The youngster was allowed freedom of movement, and stress was placed on responsibility for returning materials to their proper place when not in use, and completing a task once begun. Montessori's approach utilized the adult as director of activities rather than as teacher. This approach has been most often used with preschool education of normal children, but was built upon her experiences and intent to educate the retarded.

Institutional Growth

During the early part of the nineteenth century, various institutions for the handicapped were built and established throughout
Europe and the United States. Physicians were in charge of these
institutions. The first institution in the United States was established for the blind and the deaf. In 1848 Dr. Hervey Wilbur of
Massachusetts turned his country home into an institution for the
retarded. The same year Massachussetts opened the first state-
operated institution for the mentally retarded under the super-
intendency of Dr. Samuel G. Howe—already a recognized leader
for his work with the Perkins Institution for the Blind. Institutions
were established in New York in 1851 and Pennsylvania in 1853.

TABLE 1   Institutions for the Mentally Retarded Established in the
United States before 1900

State	Date
Massachusetts	1848
New York	1851
Pennsylvania	1853
Ohio	1857
Connecticut	1858
Kentucky	1860
Illinois	1865
Iowa	1877
Indiana	1879
Minnesota	1879
Kansas	1881
California	1885
Nebraska	1887
New Jersey	1888
Maryland	1888
Michigan	1895
Montana	1896

SOURCE: From Bill R. Gearhart and Freddie W. Litton, *The Trainable Retarded: A
Foundations Approach* (St. Louis: C. V. Mosby Company, 1975), p. 7.

Other states followed their lead, and by 1896 approximately fifteen other institutions had been established in Ohio, Connecticut, Kentucky, Illinois, Iowa, Indiana, Minnesota, Kansas, California, Nebraska, New Jersey, Maryland, Michigan, and Montana.

Gearhart reports that after the turn of the twentieth century, all but four states had public facilities or institutions for the mentally retarded. These early facilities were known by as many names as were the mentally retarded. Institutions were variously called schools, training schools, asylums, homes, and institutions. Terms used to refer to the mentally retarded included feebleminded, idiots, imbeciles, and morons.

The early leaders in schools or institutions for the handicapped were forerunners of the modern-day concepts of least restrictive environment, mainstreaming, and normalization. The primary goal of the instructional programs in these early educational environments was to remediate the mentally retarded so that they would be able to return to and function in the normal society. Soon after, these institutions changed the focus of treatment from remediation to custodial care and became warehouses for the mentally ill, the retarded, and the physically handicapped.

M. Stephen Lilly notes that commitment to these residential institutions was often required by court order. This helped increase the population of persons in institutions. As institutional centers expanded throughout the country, the change from remedial programs to custodial treatment grew. He also notes that educational programs for the handicapped in the United States were affected when public education became mandatory instead of permissive in the majority of the states. The compulsory attendance laws brought about a major difference in the type of child who attended America's public schools to include youth from all socioeconomic and cultural groups. The schools were required to adjust to accommodate children with varying instructional needs. For the first time children were included whose handicaps were not so severe as to require them to be institutionalized, but who would not be able to profit from regular educational programs. The first public school class for the mentally retarded was established in Providence, Rhode Island, in 1896. The first public school special education class met with considerable pessimism and skepticism.

A development in France during the early years of the twentieth century aided in determining which children would be enrolled in such classes. At the request of the French government, Theodore Simon and Alfred Binet developed a test to predict which children would be able to achieve in school. In 1905 these two individuals published the first individualized intelligence tests. Attention to the test in the United States was pronounced. It was translated into English and revised and standardized on American youth. The major result was the publication in 1916 of the Stanford-Binet Intelligence Test. This test has undergone a number of revisions and is still used today. The use of tests allowed schools to identify children who would not fit into regular school classes, and to diagnose them as mentally retarded for placement in special classes for the mentally retarded.

Twentieth-Century Expansion, 1900-1960

The early public school classes for the mentally retarded in the United States often enrolled students with problems other than mental retardation. It is important to note that the model for diagnosis of handicap was medical, that is, something within the child was causing the problem. This model persists today although there have been extensions of the nature and kind of information used to make the diagnosis along with alternative models of diagnosis.

Early classes for handicaps other than mental retardation included programs for the deaf, blind, orthopedically handicapped, speech defective, partially sighted, hard of hearing, and for those with chronic health problems such as malnourishment, pretuberculosis, and epilepsy.

Gearhart reports that a number of states passed laws designed to establish special classes and/or schools for the handicapped in the early twentieth century. Some of these states provided financial support for the statutes. Hewett states that by 1922 approximately 23,000 children were enrolled in public school classes for the mentally retarded. Expansion of classes for the various handicapping conditions was also influenced in the early twentieth century by recognition of new conditions requiring special education, and changes in thought about residential programs for other handicaps. For example, it was thought blind children could be educated in regular schools and would not require isolation in an institutional setting. Sigmund Freud's research in the area of emotional problems resulted in an awareness of the need for treatment of childhood emotional disturbances.

Lilly describes the period from 1925 to 1960 as one of expansion of special education. He notes that administrative innovations appeared in the operation of special classes. Among these new approaches were the itinerant special teacher, who traveled between schools to service special children for part-time instruction, and the resource room teacher, who served a particular type of handicapped child for the part of the school day when the child was not in the regular classroom.

Gearhart discusses several positive and negative factors which have influenced program development for the handicapped in the present century.

FINANCIAL CONSIDERATIONS. The special class cost was higher than that of the regular class. Most states placed a ceiling on the number of students to be served in the special class.

ADMINISTRATIVE CONCERNS. The development and maintenance of special classes was especially difficult in small, rural school districts. Other problems dealt with available teaching personnel, transportation, and grouping for instruction.

SECONDARY LEVEL PROGRAMS. Classes at the high school level were slow to develop. The academic expectations rarely exceeded upper elementary levels and there was uncertainty about the type of program to provide adolescents.

PARENT SUPPORT. Parent advocacy groups promoted the development and expansion of public school classes. This was true particularly for the trainable retarded.

MANDATORY LEGISLATION. Prior to Public Law 94-142, several states enacted mandatory special education legislation to include the more severely handicapped.

Lilly notes other factors which promoted the expansion of special education. One of these was the recognition of mild emotional disturbance or behavior disorders in children, particularly in boys. These programs grew due to the problem of appropriate settings. The children were too disruptive to regular classes, but their IQ scores were too high to be included in classes for the mentally retarded.

A second factor noted by Lilly was the nomenclature of programs for the retarded. The use of grouping—diagnosing mental retardation as educable mental retardation (EMR) or trainable mental retardation (TMR)—allowed schools to determine for a number of decades that their responsibilities were for EMR only. Most public schools imposed minimum entrance requirements, such as the child having to be toilet trained, ambulatory, and able to understand oral language. Children not meeting such stipulations were barred from attendance in public schools. Thus, TMR children were excluded and EMR children were included. So the period saw stable growth in EMR programs.

A significant factor in the expansion of special classes was the development of university teacher preparation programs, especially in the 1950s. The result was an availability of specially trained teachers to provide special education for the growing number of identified handicapped children. This growth was particularly noted in the area of mild retardation or EMR. Lilly reported that during this decade the number of classes begun for the EMR "figuratively exploded."

Action is the key word to characterize the time period beginning in the early 1960s that continues into the 1980s. Action occurred in various areas, for instance, federal government support for research, personnel preparation, and legislation; the development of a new category of exceptionality—learning disabilities; litigation in the state and federal courts; the normalization movement; child advocacy programs; mainstreaming; due process safeguards; program development for the severely handicapped; research into prevention and intervention; the efficacy of special education; and questioning of the categorical approach to diagnosis and treatment. The field of educating handicapped children is in a dynamic state which is not likely to stabilize before the twenty-first century.

Questions not yet generated relative to these action areas will influence the education of handicapped children during the next few decades. The influence of modern technology, the long-range influence of the civil rights for the handicapped movement, and the general state of modern man's quest for solutions to his problems—economic, political, and social—make the future of special education and of handicapped children both exciting and cautious. So many influences acting simultaneously will doubtless cause change, but dealing with the complexities of change dictates sobriety and careful investigation.

The emergence of the role of the federal government is the single most active force that has influenced special education in our recent history. The role of the federal government extends to policy-making and financing education for the handicapped. It has created a national "new center" since the regulations and policies it operates extend into all phases of human services—employment, due process, health and safety standards, and psychological testing, to name a few.

The impetus for this activity dates from the establishment in 1961 by President John F. Kennedy of the President's Panel on Mental Retardation. The panel prepared a report which recommended a comprehensive plan to combat mental retardation in the nation. The plan proposed that "to attack a problem as pervasive and intertwined with fundamental social conditions as mental retardation, we must think and plan boldly."[2] And bold it became. President Kennedy and his panel initiated the present federal leadership of services and treatment for the handicapped.

This strong involvement was continued by President Lyndon B. Johnson, who in 1966 appointed the President's Committee on Mental Retardation to advise him of the state of services for the retarded, to recommend areas needing federal attention, and to engage in a campaign to promote public recognition and under-standing. National legislation passed during this period included Public Laws 85-926 and 88-164. Public Law 85-926 authorized grants to state education agencies and institutions of higher learn-ing to prepare teachers for the mentally retarded. Public Law 88-164 expanded the personnel preparation of special educators for the "mentally retarded, hard of hearing, deaf, speech impaired, visually handicapped, seriously emotionally disturbed, crippled, or other health-impaired children. . . ."[3] Public Law 88-164 also mandated research and demonstration projects in the education of the handicapped.

A short-lived result of this legislation was the establishment of the Division of Handicapped Children and Youth for the administration of all existing programs for the handicapped. Public Law 89-10, the Elementary and Secondary Act of 1965, resulted in a reorganization of the U.S. Office of Education which dismantled the Division of Handicapped Children and Youth. Reaction to this administrative decision was strong among the special education profession and among parents of the handicapped. Congress, convinced by the push for the need for such a federal commitment, passed Public Law 89-750 which added Title VI to Public Law 89-10. This amendment mandated the creation of the Bureau of Education for the Handicapped (BEH). It also included regulations for preschool programs for the handicapped and the establishment of a National Advisory Committee on Handicapped Children. The Committee was charged with advising the Commissioner of Education regarding the national needs and priorities for the handicapped.

A major result of the Committee's work was the endorsement of a new handicapped condition to be recognized and to be the recipient of federal support. Part G of Title VI was passed as Public Law 91-230, the Children with Learning Disabilities Act. A few states had already begun to recognize learning disabilities as a condition and textbooks had begun to appear with learning disabilities as a primary area of concern and attention. The impact of the field of learning disabilities was to be a serious one since the field of special education had begun to reexamine the areas of educable mental retardation and behavior disorders with regard to instructional programs and teaching strategies. This reexamination was partly prompted by the attention in the field of learning disabilities to individual learning styles, personal strengths and weaknesses, and by a new administrative arrangement. Serious questions were asked with regard to the appropriateness of programs for the mildly mentally retarded and the mildly emotionally disordered. The trend began that suggested that individuals with these two problems needed more personalized attention in diagnosis and treatment vis-à-vis the learning disabilities approach.

Two other pieces of federal legislation, Public Laws 93-112 and 93-380, significantly influenced the nature of educational services for the handicapped. Public Law 93-112, the Rehabilitation Act of 1973, contains Section 504 which specifically addresses the handicapped. That section contains far-reaching implications for the handicapped that extend beyond education to civil rights. Section 504 states that "no otherwise qualified handicapped individual . . . shall, solely by reason of his handicap, be excluded from the participation in, be denied the benefits of, or be subjected to discrimination under any program or activity receiving federal financial assistance."[4] This law extended the protection afforded the handicapped to private facilities and to post-secondary education. The result was that education for the handicapped was no longer limited to elementary and secondary public schools. It extended to employment practices and program accessibility. Truly, this legislation became a "civil rights bill for the handicapped." Section 504 has not affected the nation as quickly as subsequent legislation, Public Laws 93-380 and 94-142, because it was not signed into law until April 1977. But its impact will be long-lasting and permanent.

Public Law 93-380 contained amendments that served to cover various aspects of education for the handicapped that had been addressed by the courts and that would provide an umbrella for all previous legislation. Public Law 93-380 required the states to plan for all handicapped children, to provide due process rights for the children and their parents with regard to placement in programs for the handicapped, and to guarantee that mainstream education would be provided as much as possible. It was a preface to the more extensive legislation of Public Law 94-142, the Education of All Handicapped Children Act of 1975.

While Public Law 94-142 was the culminating event of the 1970s, much of the preparation for it occurred during the 1960s and early 1970s in the form of litigation, state mandatory legislation, increased public support of services for the moderately and severely handicapped, controversy surrounding the issues of disability labels, and the efficacy of special education classes in providing appropriate services.

Litigation

Two major lawsuits provided the impetus for litigation concerning the rights of the handicapped. The inequities of the nation's system of special education were exposed through issues brought by the suits known as *Pennsylvania Association for Retarded Children* (PARC) v. *Commonwealth of Pennsylvania* and *Mills* v. *Board of Education of the District of Columbia*. The PARC suit questioned educational policies of the state of Pennsylvania that allowed the denial of services at public expense for the moderately and severely retarded. *Mills* applied to all handicapped children denied equal education opportunity. From these two cases Reed Martin has identified ten basic wrongs to be righted. Virtually all later cases and subsequent legislation for the handicapped respond to these ten basic wrongs. These wrongs are discussed below.

1. Exclusion from instruction. State laws allowed local schools to determine which students could benefit from the curriculum offerings of that school. Schools might include programs for certain types and levels of disability, but could elect to exclude.
2. Identification. Schools could choose which students to identify and to attempt to qualify for special education services.
3. Inadequate programming. Students received inadequate programs of special education for a variety of reasons which included suspension or explusion, transfers among and between programs, and interruptions inappropriate to meet student needs, such as summer vacations.
4. Inadequate or incomplete evaluations. Assessment typically consisted of testing by one individual basing placement decisions on a single criterion such as IQ socre. This resulted in significant disproportionate minority-group memberships that were often the result of discriminatory evaluation.
5. Lack of accountability. No specific goals were established for special educational programs. Student progress was not called for and seldom questioned.

6. Segregation. Students in special programs were usually segregated from the nonhandicapped. Programs were often in separate facilities on a regular campus or were in separate facilities away from regular school campuses.
7. Lack of related services. Many services the handicapped need in order to profit from special education were not provided by the public schools.
8. Failure to notify parents of changes in programs. Schools often failed to notify parents whenever changes in the identification, evaluation, or placement of handicapped children took place.
9. Records were confidential and unavailable. Parents were often not provided access to or given rights to review the confidential records of their child.
10. No due process procedure was provided. Whenever parents had a reason to challenge decisions regarding their handicapped made by the schools there was no forum to do so.

A cursory review of federal court dockets would support the litigative effort that continues relative to these ten basic wrongs. Recent decisions, in the process of appeal, have dealt with such issues as the use of intelligence tests to identify children from minority cultures as retarded, and the issue of twelve-month uninterrupted education for the severely and profoundly handicapped. Court responses to such matters have not been finalized, leading the nation into the 1980s well aware of the power of the courts to establish change in the process of education for the handicapped when leadership has not been provided by public policymakers.

State Mandatory Legislation

Lilly notes that since 1960 a significant number of states mandated special education services for the handicapped. This did not always result in special education for all handicapped youth because of failures to enforce the legislation at the local district level or to provide necessary monetary support to enact the legislation.

State mandatory legislation did, however, establish special education as a right of children rather than a privilege. This right would be addressed by Public Law 94-142 in its mandate for a free and appropriate education for all handicapped children.

Public Support for the Moderately Handicapped

School systems providing special education for certain types of handicapped youth began during the 1960s to provide alternative education programs for those who otherwise were educated in private day school programs or institutions. Exclusion was still the rule for the more severely and profoundly handicapped, but it is noteworthy that the scope of public school responsibility was expanding as the moderately handicapped began receiving services by local school districts.

Controversy over Disability Labels

Lilly notes four major factors that contribute to the controversy surrounding the continued use of disability labels as the basis for educational planning and provision of services. This controversy centers around the critical reexamination of categorical labels for children with "mild handicaps" such as educable mental retardation, behavior disorders, and learning disabilities. The first factor concerns the continued use of intelligence tests to identify the retarded. Charges are based in the claims that such measures are racially and socioeconomically biased and do not provide an adequate measure of the abilities of these children. The second factor is the obvious disproportionate number of such children in programs for the educable retarded. A third factor is the acknowledgment by many that the disability labels serve only to fill an administrative need and were not used to plan appropriate instruction. The fourth factor is the establishment of learning disabilities as a separate category of handicapped children. Many professionals consider it appropriate to use learning disabilities as an opportunity to reorganize and restructure the administrative and instructional bases of special education. The thinking is that learning disabilities should be considered a concept, not a category of exceptionality.

The learning disabilities movement emphasizes that intra-individual differences are important in planning instructional programs. All similarly labeled individuals do not need the same curriculum or instructional program. Attention is on functional abilities and not categorical characteristics.

Efficacy of Special Classes

During the 1960s noted professionals in the field of educable mental retardation began to question the appropriateness of service delivery to the EMR. The reviews of literature done at the time did not support the assumed superiority of special classes relative to academic achievement or social acceptance. The question of the most advantageous placement for the mildly handicapped has not been settled and the arguments continue. Public Law 94-142 provided some alternatives to the controversy by requiring that each child be educated in what would be the "least restrictive environment."

Public Law 94-142

To assure that the appropriate educational needs of handicapped youth are provided, Public Law 94-142 declared that all handicapped children, regardless of the type or degree of severity of the handicap, have a right to a free, public education. The mandate's design detailed many salient requirements to be met by state and local education agencies. The law was authorized as permanent legislation with no fixed expiration date. Its far-reaching implications will be felt by all sectors of the educational community for an indefinite period of time. That it encourages and emphasizes parental participation in its implication adds a dynamic thrust to its authority.

The law was signed by President Gerald R. Ford on November 29, 1975. It has already fostered considerable concern by school administrators, regular educators, and special educators. Its impact on the courts has been significant. Its influence on program changes for the handicapped has been outstanding. It will continue to assert itself within these issue areas because it requires equal educational opportunity for a subgroup which had been denied that opportunity. It is a law that supports the axiom that change is inevitable. As stated in the *Federal Register*, p. 42474 of August 23, 1977, the legislation is designed to assure that all handicapped children have available to them a free appropriate public education; to assure that the rights of handicapped children and their parents are protected; to assist states and localities to provide for the education of handicapped children; and, to assess and assure the effectiveness of efforts to educate such children.

The mandate applied to all handicapped children requiring special education and related services. Handicapped children, as defined by the act, include children who are "mentally retarded, hard of hearing, deaf, orthopedically impaired, other health impaired, speech impaired, visually handicapped, seriously emotionally disturbed, or children with specific learning disabilities."[5] These handicapped children are to receive special education and related services at no cost to parents or guardians and in the least restrictive environment for each individual child. The least restrictive environment provision required that "to the maximum extent appropriate" the handicapped child would be educated with nonhandicapped children. The management tool for framing the appropriate special education for each handicapped child in the least restrictive environment is the IEP. If developed and followed appropriately, the IEP insures that the unique needs of the child are being met. It further provides a method for monitoring the delivery of such services. The provisions of Public Law 94-142 must be adhered to by both state and local education agencies. There is no choice with regard to meeting the statutory requirements of Public Law 94-142. A summary of the critical stipulations is provided by Joseph Ballard and Jeffrey Zettel. These stipulations include:

1. Assurance of the availability of a free, appropriate public education for all handicapped children, such guarantee of availability no later than certain specified dates;

2. Assurance of the maintenance of an individualized education program for all handicapped children;

3. A guarantee of complete due procedural safeguards;

22   Austin W. Bunch

4. The assurance of regular parent or guardian consultation;

5. Assurance of special education being provided to all handicapped children in the "least restrictive" environment;

6. Assurance of nondiscriminatory testing and evaluation;

7. A guarantee of policies and procedures to protect the confidentiality of data and information;

8. Assurance of an effective policy guaranteeing the right of all handicapped children to a free, appropriate public education at no cost to parents or guardian;

9. Assurance of a surrogate to act for any child when parents or guardians are either unknown or unavailable or when such child is a legal ward of the state."[6]

Legal mandates are fulfilled not by rhetoric but by action. Therefore, Public Law 94-142 will be as strong as the American education system makes it. As posited by Martha McCarthy and Linda Marks, "this massive and permanent piece of legislation could pose one of the greatest opportunities to effect school reform witnesses to date. . . .Will P.L. 94-142 result in additional broken promises or will it signal a new era in safeguarding the rights of *all* children?"[7]

If implemented and funded as it was designed, Public Law 94-142 will be looked back upon as one of the most important events in the history of educating the handicapped. It leads our handicapped children and youth into the technological twenty-first century with a commitment by American society to provide them equal education opportunity.

Notes

1. Bill R. Gearhart and Freddie W. Litton, *The Trainable Retarded*, p. 3.

2. President's Panel on Mental Retardation, *Report to the President: A Proposed Program for National Action to Combat Mental Retardation* (Washington, D.C.: Government Printing Office, 1962), p. 12.

3. P. J. Burke, "Personnel Preparation," p. 144.

4. *Federal Register* 42: 22676.

5. Ibid., p. 42478.

6. Joseph Ballard and Jeffrey Zettel, "Public Law 94-142 and Section 504," p. 184.

7. Martha M. McCarthy and Linda G. Marks, "The New Law," p. 70.

References

Ballard, Joseph, and Zettel, Jeffrey. "Public Law 94-142 and Section 504: What They Say About Rights and Protections." *Exceptional Children* 44 (November 1977): 177-84.

Burke, P. J. "Personnel Preparation: Historical Perspectives." *Exceptional Children* 43 (November 1976): 144-47.

Federal Register 42 (1977): 22676-92 and 42474-518.

Gearhart, Bill R. *Special Education for the 80s.* St. Louis: C. V. Mosby Company, 1980.

———, and Litton, Freddie W. *The Trainable Retarded: A Foundations Approach.* St. Louis: C. V. Mosby Company, 1975.

Hewett, Frank M., and Forness, Steven R. *Education of Exceptional Learners.* 2d ed. Boston: Allyn and Bacon, 1977.

Lilly, M. Stephen. *Children with Exceptional Needs: A Survey of Special Education.* New York: Holt, Rinehart, and Winston, 1979.

McCarthy, Martha M., and Marks, Linda G. "The New Law: A Challenge for State and Local Administrators." *Viewpoints: Bulletin of the School of Education, Indiana University* 53 (March 1977): 57-71.

Martin, Reed. *The Impact of Current Legal Action on Educating Handicapped Children.* Champaign, Ill.: Research Press Company, 1980.

President's Panel on Mental Retardation. *Report to the President: A Proposed Program for National Action to Combat Mental Retardation.* Washington, D.C.: Government Printing Office, 1962.

Ryor, John. "Integrating the Handicapped." *Today's Education* 66 (September-October 1977): 24-26.

Wallin, J. E. *Education of Mentally Handicapped Children.* New York: Harper & Row, 1955.

Whitney, A. E. "The E.T.C. of the Mentally Retarded." *American Journal of Mental Deficiency* 59 (July 1954): 13-25.

2

FEDERAL LEGISLATION

Kieth C. Wright

On November 29, 1975, President Ford signed Public Law 94-142, the Education for All Handicapped Children Act. While some of its provisions may be regarded as revolutionary, the act really evolves out of a long struggle by handicapped citizens and their advocates to redress an inequity in their lives. The law establishes a formula in which the federal government makes a commitment to pay a gradually escalating percentage of the national average expenditure per public school child times the number of handicapped children served in the school districts of each state. That percentage will escalate on a yearly basis until 1982 when it will become a permanent 40 percent for that year and all subsequent years.

	Formula Scale
Fiscal 1978	5 percent
Fiscal 1979	10 percent
Fiscal 1980	20 percent
Fiscal 1981	30 percent
Fiscal 1982	40 percent

Further, the law deals with the potential threat of overcounting handicapped children in order to generate the largest possible federal allocation. The measure prohibits counting more than 12 percent as handicapped served within the total school-age (five through seventeen) population of the state.

Priorities are established which include first priority to children "unserved" and second priority to children inadequately served when they are severely handicapped. These priorities are to be adhered to by both the state and local education agencies.

Principles of Public Law 94-142

Ann P. Turnbull, B. B. Strickland, and J. E. Brantley list six principles of Public Law 94-142: zero reject, nondiscriminating testing, individualized educational program, least restrictive environment, due process, and parent participation, which are discussed below.

1. Zero Reject. *All* handicapped children are to be provided with a free appropriate public education which Section 602(18) of the law defines: Special education and related services which (a) have been provided at public expense, under public supervision and direction, and without charge, (b) meet the standards of the state educational agency, (c) include an appropriate preschool, elementary, or secondary school education in the state involved, and (d) are provided in conformity with the individualized educational program required under Section 614 (A)(5). All handicapped children are to be able to participate in all educational programs including nonacademic and extracurricular areas such as guidance counseling, sports, interest groups, and school sponsored clubs.

2. Nondiscriminating Testing and Evaluation. Severe criticisms have been leveled at the usual battery of standardized evaluation tools and the way they are given. The regulations emphasize that test procedures must be administered in the child's native language or mode of communication, must be validated, must be administered by trained personnel, must assess specific educational needs (not merely IQ), must take into account the child's impairment of senses, manual, or speaking skills, and must not be used as a single procedure to

place children. The evaluation is to be conducted by a multi-disciplinary team and that evaluation must assess the child in all areas related to the suspected difficulty.

3. The Individualized Educational Program. Public Law 94-142 requires the development of an individual written education program for each and every handicapped child served within a given state, to be designed initially in consultation with parents or guardian, and to be reviewed and revised as necessary, but at least annually (a) each child requires an educational blueprint custom-tailored to achieve the individual's maximum potential, (b) all principals in the child's educational environment, including the child, should have the opportunity to provide input in the development of an individualized program of instruction and (c) individualization means specifics and timetables for those specifics and the need for periodic review of those specifics—all of which produces greatly enhanced fiscal and educational accountability. This program of "plan," which will be discussed in detail later in the book, is the means of assuring that specific, measurable plans are developed, implemented, and evaluated for each handicapped child. The IEP forms the center of the Public Law 94-142 program. The main point is that all instruction is to be specifically designed to meet the needs of the child. Any modifications required in regular curriculum content, modes of presentation, or formats of materials will require the development of an IEP. Another important aspect of IEP development is the requirement that parents (as well as the child where appropriate) be involved in the IEP meetings and discussions about their child.

4. Least Restrictive Environment. All handicapped children are to be placed in the same educational environment as children who are not handicapped to the greatest possible extent. Since children will need a variety of placements and a variety of services, each agency is to provide a "continuance" of services which range from restricted to totally nonrestricted environment. Every effort is to be made to place children in increasingly nonrestricted environments in line with the goals of their IEP.

5. Due Process. The provisions of previously existing law
toward the guarantee of due-process rights with respect to the
identification, evaluation, and educational placement of all
handicapped children within each state are refined in Public
Law 94-142 with the following objectives: to strengthen the
rights of all involved; to conform more precisely to court
decrees; to clarify certain aspects of existing law; to guarantee
the rights of all parties relative to potential court review; to
ensure maximum flexibility in order to conform to the varying due-process procedures among the states. The law
recognizes that educators and parents are accountable for the
educational decisions made about handicapped children.
Either party or parties may initiate a due-process hearing
where complaints may be heard about the child's evaluation,
placement, or other education decisions. All parties may have
access to counsel. There is an appeal route to the state education agency if anyone is dissatisfied. The regulations give
school agencies and state agencies limited time in which to
respond and reach decisions.

6. Parent Participation. Parents are encouraged to be involved
in the whole process of education. Parents may seek independent evaluations at public expense. They are to be provided with notices of all planning, review, and due process
meetings. They have access to local educational records, and
confidentiality of records is to be insured. State plans for
special educational services are to be reviewed in public hearing with sufficient prior notice.

Events Leading up to the New Law

The struggle for an adequate public education for all children is
usually traced back to the 1954 *Brown* v. *Board of Education* case,
which ruled that although there is no federal constitutional provision for compulsory or voluntary public education, once a state
has undertaken to provide public education, it must be provided
for all. All children have not received such services. Douglas Biklen
estimated in 1976 that about 2 million children were excluded from
school and that as late as 1969 approximately 60 percent of the

mentally retarded received no education at all. Included in the statement of findings and purposes of the congressional hearing on Public Law 94-142 are these facts: more than half of the eight million handicapped children in the United States do not receive appropiate educational services; one million children are excluded entirely from the public school system; many handicapped children never have their handicaps detected during their educational experience. The Bureau of Education for the Handicapped predicts that of the two and one-half million handicapped youth to leave our school systems in the next four years, 21 percent will be fully employed; 40 percent will be underemployed and at the poverty level; 8 percent will be in their home community and idle much of the time; 26 percent will be unemployed and on welfare; and 3 percent will be totally dependent and institutionalized.

The basic principle of equal opportunity for education established by *Brown* was taken up by the federal courts in two other cases, *Pennsylvania Association for Retarded Children* v. *Commonwealth of Pennsylvania* and *Mills* v. *Board of Education of the District of Columbia*. The Pennsylvania case, decided by consent decree, established that all children are educable in one fashion or another:

> It is the Commonwealth's obligation to place each mentally handicapped child in a free, public program of education and training appropriate to the child's capacity, within the context of a presumption that, among the alternative programs of education and training required by the statute to be available, placement in a regular school class is preferable to placement in a special school class.[1]

The consent decree also established notification and due process hearings prior to any denial of admission to a public school program.

In 1972, the *Mills* decision emphasized that the Board of Education was obligated to provide whatever specialized educational services that would benefit the child. The decision clearly forbids the denial of education to any child on any basis, including lack of funds, and provides for prior hearings, periodic reviews of the child's status, and hearings prior to reassignment. "The District of Columbia shall provide to each child of school age a free and suitable publically supported education regardless of the degree of the child's mental, physical, or emotional disability or impairment."[2]

Major Aspects of the New Law

Three major aspects of Public Law 94-142 are preschool programs, individualized educational programs, and normalization.

Preschool Programs

Preschool programs are mandated by the law which requires that educational services be provided for all handicapped children between the ages of three and twenty-one. A financial bonus is provided to states that find and provide educational services in the preschool years. With almost all disabilities which handicap children, it is crucial to identify the specific disability and begin educational (and perhaps medical) treatment at the earliest possible date. For the first time, federal law requires the school system to seek out those children who may have handicaps and to begin the process of educational planning and programming by the age of three years. The law changes the role of the school system from that of a receiver of children who are chronologically old enough for school to that of a finder of children who may require individualized educational plans by the age of three.

Many readers will be familiar with the "child find" programs of various educational systems which attempt a broad campaign of parent and public education, and provide community-based diagnostic services. Early detection of disabilities can help children from becoming so handicapped by their disability that they cannot benefit from educational programs. A wide variety of screening tests and activities have been designed to assist parents, nursery teachers, and home visitors in the identification of handicapping conditions. The thrust of finding the children and providing screening and educational services moves our society from the concept of "rehabilitation" toward the concept of "habilitation," by which is meant the treatment of disabilities from birth, rather than the familiar later discovery and retraining processes. If the United States follows the example of the Scandinavian countries, there is reason to hope that initial screening would begin with the identification of high-risk mothers during pregnancy and a careful disabilities screening and treatment prescription for "found" children in the neomatch phase.

Much learning takes place during the early years, and the identification and treatment of handicapping conditions as early as possible means that found children may not have to suffer needlessly because of undetected disabilities. The Charlotte, North Carolina child find program recently found a seventeen-year-old totally deaf child who had never been to school and who had no means of communication beyond his immediate family.

It may be important to distinguish between "finding" handicapped children and "labeling" such children.

First, these children are usually placed in programs separated from "non-handicapped" children and isolated from the mainstream of school life. . . . Second, there is a terrible stigma to being labeled mentally retarded. Parents reported that their children were ashamed to be seen entering the "MR" room because they were often teased by other children about being "MRs". . . . Third, curriculum in the classes in which these children were placed is generally so limited that many children rapidly become educationally retarded, relative to children the same age who remained in the regular program . . . and fourth, these children tend to be placed permanently in classes for the mentally retarded. Our study showed that only one child in five is ever returned to the regular class.[3]

Public Law 94-142 recognizes that many testing procedures and processes for screening can be culturally and linguistically biased, and urges recognition of the "means of communication" appropriate to the child. Past experience with educational identification and placement decisions indicates that labels have been wrongly assigned to children and that the child and the parents have been stuck with the label on a fairly permanent basis.

Another major problem with labeling of children has to do with the expectations of teachers and other educational personnel as soon as the label becomes known. The label often indicates to those people that the child will act in specific patterns—stereotypes based on either the teachers' previous experiences or prejudice. So, some children face a "catch-22" situation in their placement based on labels and the school systems' expectations.

J. Mercer and Nicholas Hobbs have discussed the implications of such labeling and testing practices. It is not the intent of Public Law 94-142 to create large numbers of preschool children permanently labeled into preconceived categories and "tracked" into failure on the basis of professional expectations. To avoid such possibilities, the individualized education program is introduced as part of Public Law 94-142.

Individualized Educational Programs

An Individualized Educational Program is to be developed for each handicapped child. The process of developing the IEP allows for due process procedures for parents and child, appeals and outside consultation on specially designed instructional programs, and definite time periods for each program.

The program is to be individually developed for a child, not for a group or category of children. The education defined by the program is to specify needed elements of special education service in addition to regular classroom instruction. It is called a "program" because specific measurable services which will be provided to the child are defined. It is not a plan with guidelines, from which a program could later be developed. Turnbull, Strickland, and Brantley have developed an excellent guide to the entire process of developing IEPs. Particular reference should be made to their "Part 3 - Mechanics of IEP Development and Implementation" and the excellent Appendices.

The IEP is an agreement between a representative of the local education agency qualified to offer or supervise special education, the teacher(s) of the child, the parent or guardian, and whenever possible, the child. All these people have vital information about the child and all are to contribute to the development of the needed service program. The parents have the right to know about the program possibilities, to seek outside counsel, and to disagree with specific portions of the program.

Leroy V. Goodman notes the implications of both the preschool and the individualized portion of the law. As school systems seek to provide early, individualized educational services for handicapped children, services which are measurable and cooperatively developed, we should see the demand from parents of "normal" children for similar services.

Finally, the IEPs are meant to focus on the individual child whose needs may change over time. For this reason a child may spend varying amounts of time in regular classroom situations, special classes, or separate institutions. The burden of proof is always on the school system: is the child receiving the needed educational services in the least restrictive environment possible? The common misconceptions that handicapped children will be "dumped" in regular classrooms; handicapped children are so different that they always require specially trained teachers and special resources; and handicapped children will destroy educational opportunities for regular children, need to be discussed and denied. There is no plot on the part of Congress or the handicapped citizens groups to destroy public education or to create a unique class of specially privileged children. There *is* a long-term coordinated effort to make sure that all children have as normal an educational experience as possible, and to end the isolation so long experienced by handicapped persons.

Normalization

Society's general attitudes concerning the handicapped have been summarized in *Lori Case* v. *State of California*:

> From ancient to modern times, the physically, mentally or emotionally disabled have been alternatively viewed by the majority as dangers to be destroyed, nuisances to be driven out, or as burdens to be confined. . . . Treatment resulting from a tradition of isolation has been invariably unequal and has operated to prejudice the interests of the handicapped as a minority group.[4]

In education, these social prejudices have been manifested in institutionalization, exclusion from regular schools, stereotyped classification schemes, as well as often arbitrary and even capricious placements or programming.

Public Law 94-142 together with Public Law 90-480, "Elimination of Architectural Barriers of the Physically Handicapped," as well as the "Rehabilitation Amendments of 1973" (Public Law 93-112, which resulted in the now famous 503 and 504 regulations) have all attempted to move society toward a recognition of the rights of a minority group: the handicapped citizen. The U.S. Office of Personnel Management has issued regulations for Section 501 prohibiting discrimination in federal employment, and monitors affirmative action plans in all federal agencies. The U.S. Architectural and Transportation Barrier Compliance Board has issued regulations of Section 502 requiring removal of barriers and provision of access to federally funded construction and mass transit. The U.S. Department of Labor has issued regulations for Section 503 prohibiting discrimination in private employment. Those regulations provide that any employer with a federal government contract of more than $2,500 must take affirmative action to employ and promote the qualified handicapped; all employers with contracts larger than $50,000 and which employ more than fifty persons must have written, annually updated affirmative action programs for the handicapped; and any handicapped individual can file a complaint with the U.S. Department of Labor's Office of Federal Contract Compliance if the individual feels that an employer has failed to comply with affirmative action. The U.S. Department of Health, Education and Welfare Office of Civil Rights has issued regulations for Section 504 prohibiting discrimination in education and employment by recipients of federal financial assistance. The Office of Civil Rights has recently funded a contract to assist public libraries in understanding and complying with the 504 regulation.

One essential aspect of the "500 series" should not be overlooked. The old response that discrimination against handicapped individuals does not exist can no longer be justified. Laws do not prohibit actions that never happen. The act acknowledges that discrimination does exist and proposes ways to eliminate it. Certain perplexing aspects in the regulations require clarification. One major problem is the "reasonable accommodation" to be made for the disabled worker. How much money must be spent on special equipment, building modification, or additional workers before reasonable accommodation becomes unreasonable? The employer must be able to prove that an accommodation will impose undue hardship on the program or operation before compliance can be waived. The size and type of operation are considered. For example, a small town library with a staff of three will be treated differently than a large research/academic library with a staff of seventy-five.

The *Federal Register* gives interpretations on program access:

The Department of Health, Education and Welfare has been asked by recipients conducting modest programs (e.g., libraries in rural areas, small welfare offices, day care centers and senior citizens centers): (1) Whether they must make structural changes to buildings to accommodate persons who are mobility impaired persons even though no such persons are known to live in the area. The Section 504 regulation was carefully written to require "program accessibility," thus allowing recipients flexibility in selecting the compliance means. For example, they may arrange for the delivery of their services to persons at their homes. The regulation does not require that all existing facilities or every part of an existing facility be made accessible; structural changes are not necessary if other methods are effective in making the recipient's services available to mobility impaired persons. For example, a library building in a rural area with one room and an entrance with several steps can make service accessible in several ways. It may construct a simple wooden ramp quickly and at relatively low cost; mobility impaired persons may be provided access to the library's services through a bookmobile or by special messenger service or clerical aid or any other methods that make the library resources "readily accessible." However, recipients are required to give priority to methods that offer to handicapped and non-handicapped persons programs and activities in the same setting.[5]

A Basic Legal Definition and Some Interpretations

For educational institutions which do business with the federal government or receive grant funds, the Code of Federal Regulations defines a handicapped person as an individual who has a physical or mental impairment that substantially limits one or more major life functions, has a record of such an impairment, or is regarded as having such an impairment. Major life activities are functions such as caring for one's self, performing manual tasks, walking, standing, hearing, speaking, breathing, learning, and working. Impairments may be physiological disorders and conditions, cosmetic disfigurements, or anatomical loss affecting any of the following body systems: neurological, musculoskeletal, special sense organs, cardiovascular, reproductive, digestive, genito-urinary, hemic and lymphatic, skin, and endocrine. Also covered are mental and psychological disorders such as mental retardation, organic brain syndrome, emotional and mental illness, and specific learning disabilities. The degree to which an impairment limits an individual is evaluated in terms of employability.

This definition is much broader than the traditional categories of disability which we have usually associated with visual problems, hearing difficulties, and various obvious crippling conditions. The definition covers many hidden handicaps such as cardiovascular disease, lung diseases such as emphysema and bronchitis, kidney failure, diabetes, various forms of cancer, and epilepsy, to name a few. The key issue is the willingness of individuals to be self-declared as handicapped, and the ability of those persons to be educated and utilize their skills in a creative way. Affirmative action has to do with affirming abilities, not educating the disabilities.

Questions have been raised by the United States Supreme Court decision in *Southeastern Community College* v. *Davis* in which the court rendered its first decision with regard to the regulations of Section 504 of the Rehabilitation Act of 1973. Some people feel that this decision means that educational institutions are really blameless for their past denial of access to programs and services and that these institutions are now free to select applicants without regard to their handicapping conditions.

Specifically, this decision involved Section 84.44D of the regulations which provides that colleges and universities must make adjustments to academic requirements which discriminate on the basis of handicap, unless those requirements are essential to a particular academic program, or to licensing requirements. In a letter to universities, Health, Education and Welfare Secretary Carla Harris maintained that the content of programs and admission standards must not now discriminate against qualified handicapped students or applicants. The requirements to modify either programs or admissions standards will depend on the extent to which a program of study must be modified to meet the needs of a handicapped individual and whether such a modification would change the essential character of the program. As with other such legal actions on behalf of minorities, we can expect resistance, prejudice, and attempts at legal denial. Shortly after the Supreme Court acted against Ms. Davis on the basis of their interpretation of the 504 Regulations, the Mass Transit Association filed suit to discuss efforts to create access for handicapped citizens to buses or subways. The *Davis* decision was cited as a part of their basis for a suit. As this chapter is being completed, there is a notice in the *Wall Street Journal* that the U.S. Supreme Court will hear a case involving the University of Texas and the requirement that the University supply a sign language interpreter for a hearing impaired student. The University of Texas claims that Section 504 requires taking affirmative action steps only if they do not require financial expenditures. They cite the 1979 Supreme Court decision in *Southeastern Community College* v. *Davis*. In that case the court found that a school does not have to make "substantial modifications" in its program to accommodate a handicapped student. The 5th Circuit Court ruled that the Texas case was substantially different from the Davis case since the student can obviously perform well in his chosen profession. The Supreme Court will hear the appeal of the University of Texas, *University of Texas* v. *Walter Camenish*.

When times are good and resources are viewed as limitless, our society has a record of including more and more groups in its mainstream. Now that resources are seen as limited, tax cutting efforts abound, and inflation grows each month, we can expect to see efforts to pull back from a full financial and social commitment to handicapped children. As one handicapped person said, "Just when they decided we could have a piece of the pie, someone decided there would be no dessert."

Naturally, not all court decisions are on one side. The Seventh Court of Appeals (Chicago), in *Lloyd* v. *Regional Transportation Authority*, found that "it is plain that the rights of the handicapped were meant to be enforced at some point through the vehicle of a private cause of action."[6] This finding was written into law in the 1978 Amendments to the Rehabilitation Act, Public Law 95-602 (Section 505a). The Amendments allow the handicapped person to sue to secure the enforcement of rights in the same manner as had been previously available under Title VI of the 1964 Civil Rights Act. The amendments also allow for the recovery of reasonable attorney's fees.

Through this legislation, Congress continued to refine and develop federal programs to assist handicapped persons to take a full role in society. The law authorized a new program of independent living for handicapped people, established the National Institute on Handicapped Research, and created a fifteen member national council to advise on federal policies, programs, and services affecting the handicapped. State governments are authorized to establish systems for the protection and advocacy of the individual rights of handicapped persons. The law strengthens the enforcement authority of the Architectural and Transportation Compliance Board in civil suits in U.S. District Courts. The nondiscrimination parts of 503/504 were clearly defined as applying to any program or activities of the federal government.

A pullback from full educational and economic opportunity for handicapped persons would be tragic for several groups: first of all, for handicapped children and their families, especially those who have always been left out because of the severity of their handicapping condition or because of multiple handicaps. Those who question the high cost of providing educational services, building access, or communication aids need to consider the higher economic and social costs of underemployment or unemployment for those denied such services. The long-term costs of custodial care, underemployment, "make-work" shelters, and enforced idleness are astronomical. As persons in a position to share information about handicapped citizens, media specialists should be careful that the whole economic picture is available to citizens—not just the initial costs of building access, special equipment, or other services. The economic gains of successfully trained, employed persons who happen also to be handicapped are part of the picture.

Second, it would be tragic for "normal" children and their families if the social and educational isolation of handicapped children continues. It is destructive for children and their families to live in ghettos—even when those ghettos are comprised of the "normal" population. When we isolate children from older people, we create an unreal world and children respond with distorted perceptions of what older people are like and what happens when you get old. In the same way, isolation from people who are different because of handicapping conditions can create a wide variety of stereotypes, unreasonable fears, and a poverty of experience we would do well to avoid. In the real world, people come equipped with many different characteristics, abilities, and handicaps. We can appreciate the humanity of each one if we have a wide range of experiences with people. If we are socially isolated, we deny our own amazing array of human experiences. One of our tasks is to see that our media and materials reflect the full array of human experiences, including handicapped individuals' experiences. As our library collections are evaluated so as to be nonsexist and nonracist, so should they be "nonhandicappist."

Finally, it would be tragic for our society as a whole if we deny full participation to handicapped citizens. One measure of a society is how it provides opportunities to its citizens. A society which denys rights to certain groups on the basis of physical, mental, or emotional disabilities is clearly ethically inferior to societies in which such persons have equal opportunity. Such a society also loses the contributions of a group of citizens, a cost which it may not be able to afford in the long run. No society ever has a surplus of talent or goodness; who can say what talents, skills, or values now lie buried under the past neglect of handicapped citizens? No matter what judicial decisions are made, appropriations cut, or new restrictive laws passed, the right of full participation for handicapped citizens seems self-evident. As the caretakers of written records, media specialists should be obligated to make those records available to the handicapped as well as to utilize them to the fullest for their benefit.

Notes

1. *Pennsylvania Association for Retarded Children* v. *Commonwealth of Pennsylvania.*
2. *Mills* v. *Board of Education of the District of Columbia.*
3. Jean Postlewaite, p. 43.
4. *Lori Case* v. *State of California.* Civil No. 13127, Court of Appeals, Fourth District, Calif. December 14, 1973. p. 2a.
5. *Federal Register* 43: 36034.
6. *Lloyd* v. *Regional Transportation Authority.*

References

Abeson, Alan; Block, N.; and Hass, J. "Due Process of Law: Background and Intent." In *Public Policy and the Education of Exceptional Children,* ed. Federick J. Weintraub, et al. Reston, Va.: Council for Exceptional Children, 1976, pp. 22-32.

Abeson, Alan, and Zettel, Jeffrey. "The End of the Quiet Revolution: The Education of All Handicapped Children Act of 1975." *Exceptional Children* 44 (November 1977): 112-27.

Anderson, D. R. *Instructional Programming for the Handicapped Student.* Springfield, Ill.: Charles C. Thomas, 1975.

Biklen, Douglas. "Advocacy Comes of Age." *Exceptional Children* 42 (March 1976): 308-13.

Brown v. Board of Education of Topeka, Kansas. U.S. 483 (1954).

Bureau of Education for the Handicapped. National Advisory Committee on Handicapped Children. *Programs for the Handicapped.* Washington, D.C.: U.S. Department of Health, Education and Welfare, November/December, 1979.

Children's Defense Fund. *Children Out of School in America.* Cambridge, Mass.: Children's Defense Fund, 1974.

———. *Your Rights Under the Education of All Handicapped Children Act.* Washington, D.C.: Children's Defense Fund, 1977.

Council for Exceptional Children. *Introducing PL 94-142; Complying with PL 94-142; PL 94-142 Works for the Children.* Reston, Va.: Council for Exceptional Children, 1976.

Diamond, P. "The Constitutional Right to Education: The Quiet Revolution." *Hasting Law Journal* 24 (1973): 1087-127.

Federal Register 43 (1978): 36034.

Geddes, Dolores M. *Integrating Persons with Handicapping Conditions into Regular Physical Education and Recreation Programs.* Washington, D.C.: American Alliance for Health, Physical Education and Recreation, 1977.

Goodman, Leroy V. "A Bill of Rights for the Handicapped." *Programs for Handicapped*. Washington, D.C.: Department of Health, Education and Welfare, 1976.

Hobbs, Nicholas. *The Futures of Children*. San Francisco: Jossey-Bass, 1975.

LaVor, M. L. "Federal Legislation for Exceptional Persons: A History." In *Public Policy and the Education of Exceptional Children*, Frederick J. Weintraub, et al. Reston, Va.: Council for Exceptional Children, 1976, pp. 96-111.

Lloyd v. Regional Transportation Authority. 548 F.2d. 1277 (1977).

Love, Harold D. *Teaching Physically Handicapped Children: Methods and Materials*. Springfield, Ill.: Charles C. Thomas, 1978.

_____, and Walthall, Joe E. *A Handbook of Medical, Educational, and Psychological Information for Teachers of Physically Handicapped Children*. Springfield, Ill.: Charles C. Thomas, 1977.

Mainstreaming Preschoolers. Bethesda, Md.: ERIC Document Reproduction Services, ED 164 103-ED 164 110, 1978.

Mercer, J. "Psychological Assessment and the Rights of Children." In *Issues in the Classification of Children*, ed. Nicholas Hobbs, vol. 1. San Francisco: Jossey-Bass, 1975.

Meyer, E. L. *Exceptional Children and Youth: An Introduction*. Denver: Love Publishing Co., 1978.

Mills v. Board of Education of the District of Columbia. 348 F. Supp. 886 (D.D.C. 1972).

O'Donnell, T. "Sources of Law: Right to an Equal Educational Opportunity." *Amicus* 2 (April 1977): 22-25.

Pennsylvania Association for Retarded Children v. Commonwealth of Pennsylvania. 343 F. Supp. 279 (E.D. Pa. 1972).

Postlewaite, Jean. "Mattie T. vs. Holladay: Denial of Equal Education." *Amicus* 2 (April 1977): 38-44.

President's Committee on the Employment of the Handicapped. *A Librarian's Guide to 504: A Pocket Guide on Section 504 of the Rehabilitation Act of 1973*. Washington, D.C., n.d.

Public Law 93-112, 93d Congress, Washington, D.C., September 26, 1973, Rehabilitation Act of 1973. *United States Statutes at Large*, vol. 87, pp. 393-94.

Reynolds, Maynard D., and Birch, Jack W. *Teaching Exceptional Children in All American Schools: A First Course for Teachers and Principals*. Reston, Va.: Council for Exceptional Children, 1977.

Southeastern Community College v. Davis. 99 S. Conn. 2361 (1979).

Torres, Scottie. *A Primer on Individual Education Programs for Handicapped Children*. Reston, Va.: Foundation for Exceptional Children, 1977.

Turnbull, Ann P.; Strickland, B. B.; and Brantley, J. E. *Developing and Implementing Individual Education Programs*. Columbus, Ohio: Charles E. Merrill, 1978.

Von Hippel, D.; Foster, C.; and Lonberg, J. *Civil Rights, Handicapped Persons and Education: Section 504 Self-Evaluation Guide for Pre-School, Elementary, Secondary, and Adult Education*. Washington, D.C.: Office of Civil Rights, Department of Education, August 1978.

Weintraub, Frederick J. "Understanding the Individualized Education Program (IEP)." *Amicus* 2 (April 1977): 26-30.

3

CHARACTERISTICS
OF THE
HANDICAPPED

Kieth C. Wright

Particular kinds of physical or emotional disabilities in children are turned into handicaps by the surrounding society. Jacob ten Broek and Floyd W. Matson have discussed this socially imposed barrier which has been named "handicapism" by Douglas Biklen and R. Bagdan. Leonard Kriegal points out that a particular deadening aspect of handicapism is the paternalism of the larger society which allows it to know what is good for the handicapped, make decisions for them, set the norms, and expect thanks.

As Eliza T. Dresang has pointed out, handicapped children have the same basic needs as other children and go through the same developmental stages. Their specific needs and rates of development will be influenced by their disabilities, by the ways in which those disabilities are handled by their parents, and by the ways society tends to deal with those perceived as different. As Leopold D. Lippman states:

> to meet adequately and appropriately the needs of mentally retarded and other handicapped persons in our society calls for more than patch bandages, more than sympathy, more than "charity" in the secular sense, more than tolerance and doles in favor and make-work. What it takes is a total revision of our

society's value system. Until we see the essential equality of
every human being, until we acknowledge and act on each one's
right to equal opportunity, it's all mere rhetoric.[1]

As society begins to recognize the rights of handicapped individuals through court decisions and federal laws such as Public
Law 94-142, educators face the task of finding ways to serve not
only the handicapped child, but also the family and society in
general. Educating children who have disabilities does not remove
prejudice from society or give the members of that society successful experience with handicapped people.

This chapter will consider the following categories of handicaps:
hearing impairment, visual impairment, physical handicaps,
mental retardation, learning disabilities, and emotional handicaps.

In developing resources and programs in the media center, we
need to have some understanding of these "special" children. Collections should reflect a variety of materials covering ethnic,
sexual, and handicapped subjects. The Public Library of Cincinnati
and Hamilton County's *Dealing with Difficulties: A Bibliography*
(Cincinnati: Public Library Exceptional Children's Division, 1978)
as well as the bibliography, in *Special People Behind the Eight
Ball*, by June Mullins and Suzanne Wolf may be helpful in expanding collections. Other selection aids include: Barbara H.
Baskin's and Karen H. Harris's *Notes From a Different Drummer*;
Mary Dewitt Billings's *Coping*; Patricia Bisshop's *Books About
Handicaps*; Sharon Spredemann Dreyer's *The Bookfinder*; Coralie
Moore's and Kathryn G. Morton's *Reader's Guide*; and the National Center on Educational Media and Materials for the Handicapped's *Standard Criteria*. Publication information for these
works can be found in the reference section at the end of this
chapter.

Deaf and Hearing Impaired Children

There is a wide variation in hearing loss resulting from different
causes including long-term ear infections, illnesses accompanied by
high fevers, such as rubella, meningitis, and mumps, blows to the

head and other trauma, and congenital causes of inherited hearing loss. Hearing loss may also vary between the right and left ear.

There are two basic types of hearing loss. First, conductive hearing loss, in which there is some block in the middle ear such as wax, infection, or a foreign object, or some congenital malformation of the ear itself. This type of loss may be corrected by surgical procedures. Second, sensori-neural hearing loss, which is damage to the nerve sensors between the inner ear and the brain. We do not yet have surgical procedures to repair such nerve damage. Persons wanting to know what hearing loss is like may use the Zenith Corporation's record, "Getting Through," which describes different levels and types of hearing loss. Most people have perceptibly better hearing in one ear than the other.

"Hard-of-hearing" children can usually hear speech sounds, but may have varying degrees of difficulty decoding these sounds into understandable patterns which can be used in communication. Early detection of hearing loss in infancy and early childhood is essential so that the parent can be taught techniques to encourage the child in the use of residual hearing. Such early detection may be difficult because these children's hearing loss is not easily detected. Such children are often thought of as inattentive, daydreaming, withdrawn, or problem children.

Even with early detection of hearing loss and the proper prescription and fitting of amplification equipment, the hard-of-hearing child faces two related problems: being obviously "different" because of his or her hearing aid, and the care and maintenance of this equipment. In the case of attitude about hearing aids, the teacher and media center director also face two problems: the self-image of the hearing impaired child, and the attitudes of classmates toward "that funny device."

M. Ross has suggested that the hard-of-hearing child hears and uses sound; therefore, no matter how different the speech and language skills of each individual are, the child may appear more like normally hearing children than deaf children. Many hard-of-hearing children can hear the so-called "speech frequencies" (500, 1,000, 2,000 HZ) with amplification and can use sound effectively; however, even a slight hearing loss can cause difficulties in areas of language development, understanding of the learning process in the classroom, and overall academic performance. Ross points out that, other things being equal, an increasing gap in vocabulary growth and ability to use colloquial expressions and complex sentences develop between hearing impaired children and those children with normal hearing.

Because hearing is important to language development, reading, and other academic skills, we need to be sure that the individual child has an appropriate and functioning hearing aid and that we have done everything possible to limit the extensive noise pollution which often exists in our classrooms, media centers, and social areas. Ross points out that of one hundred children who could use hearing aids, 10 to 20 percent will not have aids, 10 to 20 percent who have aids will not wear them, and only half of the remaining children will have aids that work. M. Milner has suggested means of environmental accommodations for hearing impaired people.

If teachers and media specialists are to help hard-of-hearing children, they must be aware of the hearing loss. Communication between those responsible for hearing screening and the teacher or media specialist is essential. Every teacher and media specialist in the mainstream should know the basics of hearing aid operation and cleaning maintenance. The significance of the teacher's or media specialist's attitude cannot be stressed too much. S. Barton points out that they must now reassess their roles and traditional practices, as students will check to see what their attitude toward the hard-of-hearing child will be. Often the bewildered or dismayed teacher or media specialist's attitude is perceived as negative toward such a child. Media specialists and teachers can deal with mechanical problems of hearing aids in a matter-of-fact way, can encourage the hard-of-hearing child to explain or demonstrate the use of the aid if he or she is willing, and can be sure there are books and media in the school collection which have the hard-of-hearing as characters in the stories. Hard-of-hearing children who are accepted and respected will grow to accept and respect themselves.

Teachers and media specialists need to be sensitive to the tremendous quantity of highly verbal learning situations in the classroom. All hearing impaired children will have difficulties if the major learning modality is auditory, and will need visual and indivudial reinforcement. However, we cannot modify the ways in which instruction is presented if we don't know the children are present. In some situations, an adequate hearing screening program will provide for early detection. In other situations, the teacher or media specialist will need to be aware of some of the sights of hearing difficulties such as: lack of attention to verbal instructions, or inability to follow directions; positioning the body so as to favor one ear; hesitancy to participate in large-group verbal activities; obvious problems with the ear (drainage, chronic colds) or complaints about "aches" in the ear; gross differences between observed behavior and test scores; and withdrawal from activities with other students.

"Deaf" children are unable to hear speech sounds so that they can be understood and used in the communication process. Eugene Mindel and McCoy Vernon, Peter J. Fine, and Hilde S. Schlesinger and Kathryn P. Meadow have discussed the impact of deafness and hearing impairment on the child. Since so much information about our social world comes to us by the means of the auditory channel, undetected hearing loss may mean that a child is cut off, partially or totally, from the basic socializing process, and that basic developmental foundations for language and reading success are missing.

A great deal depends on the age at which the hearing impairment occurred and the age at which it is discovered. Children who have the opportunity to hear speech and understand it prior to a hearing loss come to the school or media center with an auditory memory of language sounds and referents. If the child's parents know about the hearing loss, they can begin to seek means of communication with the child including hearing aids, special attention to the use of sounds, speaking to the child when the individual is looking at a person, and total communication, a system of sign language, sound, and lip movement.

Lee Katz, S. L. Mathis, and E. C. Merrill have summarized the issues facing parents as they consider public school education for their hearing impaired children. A basic issue lies in the area of communication. Will the child understand what is happening in the school, and will people on the school staff attempt to communicate with the child and encourage other children to do so? In the past a major argument in education of hearing impaired children centered on "oral" communication (speech reading) versus "manual" communication (some form of hand-gesture language). Obviously there is no one answer for all children. Some children can learn to speech read very well, some children need visual stimulation in terms of clear sign symbols, pictures, and other graphics. J. Z. Orlansky points out that not all learning impaired people use sign language, speech read, have understandable speech, wear hearing aids, or see so well they can overcome their hearing loss; yet, we may generalize by saying that all such people have a communication problem to some degree.

Because of this communication problem, many hearing impaired children entering school will have language deficits. They may have concepts or experiences for which they have no English-language symbol. A common fallacy is that deaf people, including children, will read extensively because they cannot hear. The English-language problem often makes reading for information or pleasure difficult.

The language problem is acute for the educational process because a language base is essential to other skills such as listening, speaking, reading, and writing. This language problem is also the source of a major myth about deaf and hearing impaired persons: because they do not use good grammar, they are not very bright. Deaf adults are often painfully aware of this English-language problem and tend to socialize only in their own community.

The media specialist needs to be aware of certain basic principles in communicating with the hearing impaired person: Talk with such persons. Never talk with your back turned, or with a fingernail, a cigarette, or anything in front of your mouth. Use complete, brief sentences, especially with children, and speak in a natural, pleasant voice without overstressing parts of words or using excessive facial expressions that make speech reading difficult. Even if you don't know sign language or fingerspelling, use natural gestures as when you talk with anyone else. Use as much body and indication language as possible. Look at, touch, point out, nod toward what is being discussed. Remember that when a hearing impaired person is facing away from you, a gentle touch will get his or her attention. Don't flap your whole arm. Always check to see that what you have communicated has actually been understood—don't take a nodded head as evidence. Use as many "visuals" as possible to illustrate what is going on. In media center programs, the staff may wish to explore use of signs and voice in what is called "total communication." Pictures, puppets, signs, and captioned films may also be used.

There are a number of materials which combine signs and stories available from the Gallaudet College bookstore (Kendall Green, Washington, D.C. 20002) and Joyce Motion Picture Co. (8613 Yolanda Ave., P.O. Box 458, Northridge, Calif. 91324). Many community colleges, universities, and adult education programs offer introductory sign language programs and courses related to the learning impaired individual. State library agencies and state departments of education will both have information on educational captioned films and other media materials for these children. Sign language systems are not only useful with the deaf child, but may also prove very effective with children who have other communication difficulties and/or deficits in intellectual functioning. The bibliography by W. P. Brown, G. C. Vanderheiden, and D. Harris illustrates the wide array of techniques and technology now in use. Lloyd's book *Communication Assessment and Intervention Strategies* contains a number of articles on nonverbal sign systems for children who have verbal communication disorders.

As media specialists begin to select materials and programs for hard-of-hearing and deaf persons, they will need to consult repeatedly with professional colleagues and with hearing impaired persons. Even current books contain much misinformation about what causes hearing loss, what it's like to be deaf, and what people should do when they come in contact with such persons. Programs and materials should provide "deaf awareness" that is accurate and assists people in overcoming their stereotypes about the disability.

Blind and Visually Impaired Children

The term "blind persons" indicates here those persons who cannot use any print format, no matter how enlarged or illuminated, for practical reading purposes; and "partially sighted persons" indicates those persons who can read if materials are modified in terms of print size or type of projection. Anne L. Corn and Iris Martinez offer definitions of common visual problems in their book on visually handicapped children in the classroom.

Blind and partially sighted persons vary in terms of the amount and type of visual loss and in terms of the age of onset. A child who has been blind since birth lacks visual memory of the world, while a child who *becomes* blind will have a far different memory of the world.

Hanan C. Selvin points out, in agreement with R. A. Scott, that the condition of "blindness" is really a learned social role. All persons who have visual impairment or are facing impending visual impairment learn to deal with it in some way. Much of their acceptance or rejection of the fact will depend not only on their own activities, but also on the reactions of family, friends, and teachers. A person can be said to be legally blind when the visual acuity with correcting lenses of that person is less than 20/200, or when his or her field of vision is less than twenty degrees. Normal (often corrected) activity is 20/20 and normal field of vision is a little over 180 degrees.

Michael Orlansky lists three types of visual impairments. *Visual acuity* may be reduced so that the child may not see sharply and may need to get very close to see objects. Wrapping gauze over the eyes or using out-of-focus binoculars will give an impression of this problem. *Field of vision* may be restricted so that the usual wide area taken in by the eye is restricted. Looking through a paper tube or paper cylinders mounted on glasses frames will give some impression of the restricted field of vision. *Color vision* may be defective. Here the contrast between black-and-white and color television may be helpful. Try watching the same program on two sets side by side. Since many warning devices such as stop lights and signs are color coded, children with color vision defects must learn other cues to "read" these messages.

Orlansky, S. McDonald and D. Parnell, P. H. Hatlen, Kenneth A. Hanninen, and E. Scott have all offered practical suggestions concerning the integration of blind and partially sighted students into the regular classroom. First, the attitude of the teacher is crucial to the students' success. Every attempt should be made to deal with these students like all other students in terms of assignments, activities, seating, and use of free time. In the beginning everyone may be uncomfortable with "visual" verbs like "see," "look," and "blind," but normal use of language should be encouraged.

Second, mobility independence is important to the success of these children. While other children or aids may have to assist the child in orientation to the room and building, the goal should be free mobility throughout the school. Kay E. Aylor has suggested that in-service training should include an experience of trying to guide a blindfolded person with verbal directions. Once children have learned the setup of a room, it will help if they are told when major furniture, lounges, shelves, or tables are moved.

Third, the teacher or media specialist should be ready to offer cues when necessary about which direction to face when speaking to a group, or where the picture under discussion is located. In the beginning it will be helpful if the teacher and students identify themselves when they are speaking. Never walk away or leave the room without telling the blind child.

Fourth, there are many devices to assist the blind and partially sighted person in the learning process. These include cassette recorders, braille equipment, enlarged texts, closed circuit television, "talking" calculators and print readers, and large-type typewriters. The available equipment should be introduced as unobtrusively as possible. Questions of other children should be answered, perhaps by the blind student, but the emphasis should be on the use of equipment by the blind or partially sighted students in the normal flow of activities, not on demonstrations for other students.

Fifth, good nonglare lighting and adjustable desk tops may be very helpful to partially sighted students. Remember that many books and kinds of paper for writing have a high glare factor. Felt tipped pens and soft lead pencils may also help the partially sighted student.

Sixth, the regular classroom environment makes much use of visual materials on chalk boards, posters, and flip charts. In helping classroom teachers with curriculum development, we should be ready to suggest alternatives for the blind and partially sighted child such as individual large drawings to be passed out instead of a sketch on the chalk board, raised-line drawing for the blind student (often hand done with the braille stylus), and special braille material available from outside sources. In general, the principle is to create classroom and media center instructional situations in which the blind or partially sighted student has access to the same information and opportunities for participation as the other students, without creating a situation where the child is held up as different.

Finally, there are numerous devices for transforming print into a usable format for the visually impaired child. Some portable devices are no more than magnifying glasses, sometimes illuminated. Beyond these are the closed circuit television reading devices.

Closed Circuit Television Reading Devices

Closed circuit television reading devices are designed to magnify printed material electronically. Their major components are a mounted camera, a self-contained light source, a lens capable of magnifying print to various sizes or one fixed to individual specifications, and a monitor (television screen). Some examples include: *Electronic Visual Aid*. Has a seventeen-inch fixed or adjustable monitor. Apollo Lasers, 2124, Model 2B (vertical camera); 4124 Model 4A (horizontal camera); 610 (two-camera, split screen combination). *LVA 500*. Equipped with self-supporting scanning table, fourteen inch monitor, and horizontal camera. Pelco Sales, Inc. *Optiscope Electro CC5000*. Has a seventeen-inch monitor and typewriter capability. Stimulation Learning Aids, Ltd. *Portareader*. Has twelve-inch monitor and typewriter capability. Apollo Lasers, 5100. *Schmidt Reader*. Portable unit with nineteen-inch monitor, from Edutrainer, Inc. *Standard Read/Write System*. Has nineteen-inch monitor. Visualtek, RS-6. *Visualtek's Commuter*. Has nine-inch monitor. Visualtek. *Visualtek's Microviewer*. Allows visually handicapped persons to view microfiche and microcards through enlarged images. Visualtek systems are also sold by Science for the Blind Products, Inc. *Visualtek's Miniviewer*. Has a twelve-inch monitor. *National Institute of Rehabilitation Engineering*. Will design closed circuit television systems based on the evaluation of an individual's visual loss or a recommendation from an eye doctor.

Practical aids for the visually impaired for almost any conceivable task are available. Catalogues available from the following organizations may be useful: Aids and Appliances

Division, American Foundation for the Blind, 15 W. 16th Street, New York, N.Y. 10011; Aids and Appliances Division, National Foundation of the Blind, 1839 Frankfort Avenue, Louisville, Ky. 40206; Howe Press, Perkins School for the Blind, Watertown, Mass. 02172.

Other Equipment

In the school media center the most important program element is the professional media specialist who has learned something about the needs of visually impaired persons and who attempts to keep abreast of the rapidly changing technology and services offered to blind and visually impaired persons. Being on the mailing lists of major organizations of blind persons and the regional library of the National Library Service for the Blind and Physically Handicapped will help in this task.

Another important program element is some means of allowing visually impaired persons to learn how the media center is arranged. A braille-labeled map, a raised-line drawing, or a scale model of the media center can be used. Braille or raised letter and number signs on doors, elevators, stack ends, boxes, and so forth are also helpful to blind individuals. In some facilities "talking" signs which respond to touch with a recorded message have been used.

Visually impaired children and adults often require special devices or other persons to act as readers. Anyone who has heard the Kurzweil machine "read" at demonstrations can appreciate the noise and annoyance factor which even the best reader will encounter. For this reason Selvin suggests the need for rooms or reading areas which are fairly soundproof, so that cassette recorders, live readers, or Kurzweil-type machines can be used freely without disturbing other users of the media center.

A major need of all visually impaired students in schools and colleges is available textbooks and required reading materials (often placed on reserve in academic libraries). The media specialist, working with the teacher, needs to make arrangements prior to the beginning of a semester or instructional unit for required materials to be available to loan to students. Recordings for the

Blind provides a recorded textbook service, but a good deal of lead time is required to get copies. Often current materials from newspapers, journals, or government reports must be recorded on site by volunteers. Where school systems have access to a Kurzweil machine, recordings of limited quality can be made inexpensively. Planning ahead with teachers is crucial; it does no good to receive required readings one week prior to the end of a semester. Regional libraries of the National Library Service have information on other organizations that record materials.

When media centers begin serving visually impaired persons, they also begin machine acquisition and maintenance. Media specialists should carefully consult with blind and visually impaired persons as well as local professionals prior to any equipment purchases. Very expensive translation technology may not be the answer in many situations. One can buy and have modified a dozen cassette recorders for the price of one such expensive device, or 150 recorders for the price of another. Let your users advise you. Once equipment is acquired, provision must be made for its periodic inspection and repair. Most media center systems have media technicians who can undertake such tasks; however, both budget and time must be allocated to this task.

A major assumption of instructional programs in America is that everyone can use their eyes to read, to see the chalk board, to use laboratory instruments, and to view media. Media specialists need to challenge this assumption and assist teachers in the process of providing access to materials, instruments, and information which can be efficiently used by blind and visually impaired persons.

Physically Handicapped Children

For the physically handicapped child, the basic problem is *access*: access to school from home (by car, school bus, walkways); access to the school building and to the rooms and resources of the school. Most older buildings and transportation systems do not provide adequate access. Edward Noahes points out that media facilities designed for the "average" person rest on three assumptions: most people possess statistically average characteristics; those who do not possess such characteristics can easily adapt to design solutions based on average characteristics; and those who cannot adapt constitute a very small percentage, are in institutions, or at least are out of sight.

Dorothy Edgington offers practical guidance for the classroom teacher who faces the prospect of having physically handicapped children in the classroom. Many of her suggestions or attitudes, management of seeing peers, and activities modifications may be helpful in the media center.

It is important to note that many people are physically handicapped on a temporary basis. Public transportation, curbs, stairs, heavy doors, or crowded rest rooms all provide barriers to most of us at some time during our lives. Accessible facilities do not benefit only the permanently handicapped.

We do know how to create accessible transportation and facilities. Following are some available resources in this area:

ABRA! *Seven Slide-cassettes on Barrier Removal for All.* (ABRA! Project, East Central University, Ada, Okla. 78420.)

Educational Facilities Laboratory, and the National Endowment for the Arts. "Arts and the Handicapped—an Issue of *Access.*" (New York: The Laboratory, n.d. (The Laboratory is located at 850 Third Ave., New York, N.Y. 10022.)

Mace, Robert. *An Illustrated Handbook of the Handicapped Section of the North Carolina State Building Code.* Raleigh: North Carolina Department of Insurance, 1974. (The department's address is P.O. Box 26387, Raleigh, N.C. 27611.)

Nugent, Timothy. *Architectural Accessibility.* Washington, D.C.: White House Conference on Handicapped Individuals Office, 1976.

President's Committee on the Employment of the Handicapped. *Making Colleges and Universities Accessible to Handicapped Persons.* Washington, D.C.: The Committee. (Reprint of "Architectural Checklist" from State University Construction Fund, Albany, N.Y., n.d.)

U.S. Department of Housing and Urban Development. *Barrier Free Site Design.* Office of Policy Development and Research in Cooperation with the American Society of Landscape Architects Foundation, 1975.

U.S. General Accounting Office. *Report to Congress: Further Action Needed to Make All Public Buildings Accessible to the Physically Handicapped.* Washington, D.C.: General Accounting Office, 1975. (Write to 441 G Street, N.W., Washington, D.C. 20548.)

Before considering physical barriers to access, media specialists may want to consider the barriers created by attitudes. Ruth A. Velleman, R. T. Sale, and Kieth C. Wright have all explored these barriers. Attitudes usually depend on the amount of information a person has about a particular group, and the amount of direct personal contact that person has with members of that group. Where accurate information is missing and contact is never established, we can expect stereotyping. We need to be alert to some possible negative attitudes.

APATHY. Apathy is usually expressed by people who are simply unaware that handicapped people exist, or who believe that if they do exist, they are cared for in special programs. If they are invisible, we don't make access possible.

PATERNALISM. Paternalism is usually expressed by well-intentioned people who believe handicapped persons need protection, permanent care, sympathy, and extra attention. They want to wrap the handicapped child in a cocoon.

FOCUS ON THE DISABILITY. A focus on the disability is usually expressed by the person who wonders, "how a person like that can possibly . . ." with emphasis on what can *not* be done rather than on the possibilities. Sometimes such a focus "spreads" to a belief that a blind person also cannot hear or walk. If one sense is disabled, all are.

FEAR OR DISCOMFORT. Fear or discomfort is usually expressed by persons with no previous contact, or one dramatic negative contact in the past, who do not know how to act or what to say in the presence of a disabled person. This combination of unreasonable fear and embarrassment can be "paralyzing."

STEREOTYPING. Stereotyping is usually expressed by persons who have strong preconceived ideas about what certain disabilities are like and what kinds of interests and lives disabled people must have. Often such stereotypes depersonalize the disabled person in the same way that sexism and racism depersonalize their victims.

Stereotyping often leads to the dissemination of "facts" about disabled persons that have no basis in reality.

Overcoming such attitude barriers in one's self and on the part of other staff members will go a long way toward removing physical barriers to access.

As physically handicapped children enter our schools, we need to consider the arrangement of our media centers so that they can be made accessible. Velleman makes the following suggestions: (1) Media center facilities should be "open" psychologically and physically so that people in wheelchairs will feel welcome and able to move about freely. (2) Shelving should not be over five feet high and is easiest to use if placed around the perimeter of the room. If there are rows of shelves, can a person in a wheelchair enter an aisle, turn, get a book, and exit? Lowest shelves may often be useless. (3) The base of a catalog cabinet should be sixteen inches high. If a book catalog is used, it should be accessible to a person in a wheel- chair, and as light as possible. Media centers going to on-line systems and microform catalogs should think about ease of retrieval by the handicapped. (4) Pages in catalogs, indexes, and reference tools should be strong enough not to tear easily. (5) Non- print materials and realia as well as pamphlet and vertical files should be arranged for ease of access. (6) Tables should be high enough so that wheelchair arms are clear when rolled up to the table. Tables with aprons or pedestal legs will block wheelchairs. Some wheelchairs are twenty-nine inches tall—can their occu- pants find a table to use? (7) Windows and bulletin boards should be low enough to be useful to those in wheelchairs. This also holds true for drinking fountains, telephones, copy machines, and change-making machines.

Many physically handicapped children can use regular print and media materials if they can get to the shelves, cabinets, and hardware, however, some children have disabilities which make use of regular print materials and media equipment impossible. Much media equipment can be modified to allow for use, and the recorded material of the National Library Service and Recordings for the Blind will help these print-handicapped individuals.

It is important to make sure that the access we create does not isolate the physically handicapped child. Ramps may be created so that everyone enters and leaves the building together; or the ramp may require the handicapped child to use a separate door, or use another route into and out of the building. Rest rooms, tables, media centers, cafeterias, gymnasiums, and school buses should all be examined to see that everyone has access. In media center operations, story telling, puppet theater, and library instruction should be evaluated to see if physically handicapped children can participate with other students in these activities.

The Mentally Retarded Individual

According to the American Association on Mental Deficiency, mental retardation has three basic characteristics: subaverage intellectual functioning, deficits in adaptive behavior, and appearance of these characteristics during the development period. This definition stresses that IQ test scores alone do not define the whole person. We need to know when these characteristics appeared, and to observe the social/adaptive activities of the individual. Many mentally retarded individuals can learn to function as productive, well-adjusted members of society. The goal of independent living is appropriate for these persons. Marc Gold has demonstrated that even very severely retarded individuals can be trained to care for themselves and to do fairly complex work tasks.

Until the 1960s, most people believed that once retarded persons reached a particular level of development, they would stay there. Educators now think that most mentally retarded persons can grow and develop. Many concrete, practical living skills are being taught to mentally retarded persons of all intellectual levels. Often this learning experience takes place through learning-by-doing.

For the media specialist, certain characteristics of these children and their educational programs are important. First, there will be disparity between chronological age and mental age. For example, the educable mentally retarded child who is seven to nine years old will have a mental age of four to six years but will not usually have begun to read. This child should be interested in reading and pictures in books, and is ready for a reading readiness program. These children can develop reading skills including reading of signs, charts, and stories from the chalk board, and can in time develop the ability to read spontaneously for information (use the telephone directory, newspapers, and dictionary), and for pleasure (read magazines, fiction, and so on). The goal is to develop the highest possible reading level on the basis of the child's interest.

Second, part of the educational program for the EMR child will include the development of living skills which will help the child adjust in socially acceptable ways within the environment of the larger community. Media centers offer programs and facilities where such skills can be developed in an open atmosphere. It is important that the media specialist cooperate closely with the teacher in order to discover what specific areas of coping skills need to be developed.

Third, educational programs and media activities need to advance at the child's pace—not at the expectation level of the teacher or media specialist. Encouragement, patience, repetition, simple statements, breaking complex tasks down into simple tasks, and short work periods matched to attention span will all help.

Fourth, some children present behavior problems in terms of hyperactivity, repetitive movements such as rocking, and other behavior which may disturb other students and/or be grossly unacceptable in social settings. It is important to try to find out the reason for the problem, again consulting with teachers and specialists. Other practical techniques include isolating the child from other children in the media center, changing the activity, trying other ways to get attention (visual, verbal, or tactile), and limiting excesses with firm, consistent discipline.

Fifth, some children will have experienced failure in the classroom and the school. They may expect to fail in the media center and come to the program with a negative frame of mind. Discovering interests through conversation and story hours, and helping to develop success-insured activities at the child's level may help. The media specialist should avoid situations which emphasize verbal or motor competition with other children. One purpose of the media center program should be to restore, or build, the confidence of the children in their own abilities ("We can do it").

Finally, some children have deficits in visual perception abilities, auditory skills, and speech. Many activities of the media center such as storytelling, sequencing of flannel board pictures, puppet activities, let's write a story, repetition of fingerplays, songs, and so on can be used to help children develop skill in all these areas.

The following specific suggestions for media specialists may be helpful.

GET TO KNOW THE INDIVIDUAL. The media staff should spend enough time with individuals to know their interests and have some estimate of their reading level. The staff needs to gain the confidence of the mentally retarded individual who may be suspicious. This suggestion does not mean that the media specialists will diagnose each individual in any clinical sense, or apply any set of standardized tests. Rather, mentally retarded individuals come with a variety of interests and needs. Media programs and services need to be matched with these needs and interests.

USE ACTIVITIES WHICH INVOLVE ALL OF THE SENSES. Beyond picture books and puppets, media activities should be developed which involve actual experiences—touching, smelling, tasting, drawing. Take group visits to nearby places. Use the story involving the gingerbread man (or another edible) followed by making, baking, smelling, and eating. Color pictures mounted on cardboard may be used for story presentations and passed among the members of the group. Any activity which involves several of the senses will be more meaningful to the participant. Media specialists may find that several objects, activities, or situations will be needed to develop the real sense of concept. Imagine several ways to deal with the concept of "big and little," "hard and soft," or "loud and quiet." Media materials for such activities can include a number of toys, found objects, and homemade devices.

MAKE USE OF CUES AND REPETITION. Story hours or puppet theater or questions in a group setting should make use of various cues suggesting appropriate answers that allow individuals to take the risk of responding. Individuals are often afraid of failure in the group setting. As the media specialist develops ongoing groups or discussions, the number of success cues can often be lessened. Repetition of a single idea, a theme, or an activity can be useful in this context. Picture books, stories, drama, records, and songs should have repeated themes that individuals come to expect, to anticipate, and finally, to modify for their own enjoyment. Success for each participant can motivate individuals to try more and more complex and involved activities. Language skills can be developed by activities such as: naming things inside and outside the immediate environment; describing what is done, seen, felt, tasted; same/different concepts (shapes, sizes, textures, sounds and meanings of words); classifying objects, people, and things with abstract words (saw and hammer are tools); sound making and experimenting; experimenting with voice changes (quality, loudness, or pitch); using speech to verbalize solutions and solve simple problems ("How would you fix it?"); teachers' use of questions, commands, instructions, comments, and so on to stimulate language; having children phrase questions to the media specialist and to each other; and encouraging children to express ideas freely by establishing a free discussion period.

INVOLVE VISUAL MEDIA. Pictures, puppets, and projected transparencies need to be used with a good sense of visual literacy. The image should be clear and uncluttered and free of complicating details. Color pictures should use bold and primary colors, and any kind of transparence should be clearly evident and outlined.

USE TOUCH AND DEMONSTRATION IN THE PROCESS OF COMMUNICATION WITH INDIVIDUALS. Many of us grew up in environments where "how to" was the regular mode of instruction. Mentally retarded individuals often have to be shown—by demonstration (do as I do), by doing it together (your hand and my hand work together), and by breaking down complex tasks into their component parts. It is important that the verbal instructions be direct and to the point.

USE CONSISTENT ACTIVITIES. The media specialist needs to remember to keep an activity going long enough for all of the participants to become involved. If possible, alternate activities should be available for those who become bored or have short attention spans. When planning programs, media specialists should avoid sudden drastic changes in activities. The individual who is enjoying a successful experience with a cassette deck may not want to stop so the room can be darkened for a film, or to join in a rhythm-based folk story. The learning center concept used in educational settings may be useful for media centers in context. Such learning centers are often used in educational settings with a variety of learning activities including spelling, reading with an individual, various language charts, chalkboard activities, using work books, math work activities, leisure time activities, art center, and audiovisual centers. Michael Bender and Peter J. Valletutti offer specific curriculum strategies and activities which might be adapted to the media center program.

Media specialists are involved in materials selection for mentally retarded persons. It may be helpful to note some specific cognitive areas and their implications for materials.

AREA	MATERIAL IMPLICATIONS
Attention	Materials need to be colorful, in bold shapes, and simple.
Comprehension of abstraction	Materials need to be simple, concrete, and free of "noisy" extraneous elements.
Progression skills	Materials should be presented in short incremental steps.
Motivation	All students need materials which can be used to give immediate and meaningful reinforcement.
Reception of information	Multisensory materials and kits involving sight, touch, smell, sound, and movement may be utilized.
Interaction	Materials should be formatted so presentation can involve teacher-child interaction.

AREA	MATERIAL IMPLICATIONS
Repetition	Materials which can be used to reinforce by repetition will help.
Success or "completion"	Materials selected should allow for successful completion—a sense of mastery.

Learning Disabled Children

The term *learning disability* was defined by the National Advisory Committee to the Bureau of Education for the Handicapped, U.S. Office of Education as follows:

> Children with special learning disabilities exhibit a disorder in one or more of the basic psychological processes involved in understanding or in using spoken or written language. These may be manifested in disorders of listening, thinking, talking, reading, writing, spelling, or arithmetic. They include conditions which have been referred to as perceptual handicaps, brain injury, minimal brain dysfunction, dyslexia, developmental aphasia, etc. They do not include learning problems which are due primarily to visual, hearing, or other handicaps, to mental retardation, emotional disturbances or environmental disadvantage.[2]

This definition assumes that the child will have average or better IQ scores and that the performance of the child will not match what might be expected from the IQ level. This major discrepancy between expected and actual performance is usually found in some part of the language activity of the child, most typically in reading difficulties.

Many children who come to school media centers have learning disabilities. What are some of the clues to these disabilities?

POOR VISUAL DISCRIMINATION. The child has difficulty distinguishing similar shapes such as squares or rectangles, circles or ovals; letters such as m and n, b and d, g and q; numbers such as 6 and 9; or the number combinations 21 and 12. The child will evidence difficulty in sequencing objects or concepts due to such discrimination problems.

POOR VISUAL MEMORY. The child may forget what he sees or may not remember what he has read. Immediate reinforcement of visual experiences may be necessary.

POOR FEELING (KINESTHETIC) SENSE. The child may not be able to feel the difference between a penny and a nickel, or a dime and a quarter. He or she may not be able to identify cutout shapes of animals or alphabet letters by feel. Larger, simpler shapes and textures in simple combinations may be useful in developing these skills. A sense of "play" or "game" in such activities will help.

POOR EYE-HAND COORDINATION. The child may have difficulties with tracing, copying, hitting a ball, or inserting a cassette or film strip. Because of poor eye-hand coordination the child may have difficulty in determining where his or her body is in relation to others, resulting in blows, running into people, or other accidental confrontations.

POOR SPACIAL ORIENTATION. The child may have difficulty remembering the difference between various spacial concepts such as left and right, up and down, over and under, outside and inside, on top of and underneath. Games which use the concepts with words, action, and music may be helpful.

POOR FIGURE GROUND DISCRIMINATION. The child may have difficulty selecting one thing from a group, such as a specific letter out of a word or series of words; "my" cubby hole as distinguished from the cubby holes of other children in the classroom; "my" chair as distinguished from the chairs of other people in the room. Flannel board, photography, and identification activities will be helpful here.

GETTING STUCK (PRESERVATION). The child may have difficulty shifting from one activity to another and may give the same answer, once he has found it is correct, to very different questions. Activities which encourage alternatives ("try it another way"), and do not stress failure will be helpful.

HYPERACTIVITY AND LETHARGY. The child may become confused, bewildered, or upset by a structured lesson or activity and talk at any time, move about, touch things, make rhythmic movements and beating noises on the table, distracting others. Such hyperactivity may be contrasted with the lethargy of a child who suddenly, after a great deal of activity, refuses to participate in activities.

Many of the problems that these children have cause them to be mislabeled as mentally retarded, stubborn, emotionally disturbed, or even bad. There are some similarities between the language processing problems of mentally retarded, hearing impaired, and learning disabled children. For this reason, it is important that these children have professional testing to determine the origin and nature of the specific problem.

The difficulties which learning disabled children experience may result in some serious distinction of attitudes about school and school work, about adults in general, and about their peers. These children have often experienced failures, not only in academic, but also in social functioning. How other people feel, what is socially acceptable, the "rules of the game" may all be mysteries to them. Such children need specific help in the following areas:

MODULATION OF BEHAVIOR. The child may over- or under-react to situations. Whatever "appropriate" behavior or function may be, the child needs assistance in developing that appropriateness.

DEALING WITH COMPLEX TASKS. The child has increasing difficulty dealing with increasingly complex tasks. Often such tasks may be broken down into less complex tasks. Integration of tasks into a complex matrix will take time.

APPROPRIATENESS OF RESPONSE. The child will tend to exaggerate responses to praise, to discipline, to new situations, to disappointments, to loss. Often such responses will offend other children and be misunderstood by adults. Identifying and encouraging appropriate responses is important.

C. Metsker's publication offers numerous activities and games for
"children who have difficulty learning" which can be adapted to
library and media center programs.

In the media center, various tools such as indexes, encyclopedias,
card catalogs, and instruction books for hardware, may be difficult
if not impossible for some learning disabled children to use. Finding
materials that are both interesting to the child and usable may be
the greatest challenge for the media specialist. For students whose
disability prevents reading, the talking book program of the National Library Service of the Library of Congress or other recorded
media may be useful. Also, try Dorothy Witrosis's *Gateways to
Readable Books: An Annotated Graded List of Books in Many
Fields for Adolescents Who Find Reading Difficult* (New York:
Wilson, 1975), and Evelyn Altum's "Books for the Young Disabled
Readers." (*School Library Journal* 98, no. 18 (1973): 3161-64). The
Public Library of Cincinnati and Hamilton County, Ohio has two
bibliographies of interest, *Books for Mentally Retarded Children*
(1973), and *High Interest Low Vocabulary Reading List* (1976).
Finally, the American Library Association has a packet entitled
"High Interest/Low Reading Level Information Packet," from a 1978
preconference, "Dispelling the High-low Blues." Careful selection
of materials keyed to the child's interest and skill levels may open
up the media center to the child's continuing use.

The Emotionally Handicapped Child

The terms "emotionally handicapped," or "socially maladjusted,"
or "mentally ill" have been used to cover a wide variety of behavior
problems in the school ranging from momentary outbursts to
long-term difficulties in which children seemingly lose contact with
themselves, their world, and the present. Samuel A. Kirk defines
these behavior disorders as those which deviate so far from age-
appropriate behavior that the behavior interferes with the
children's own development and also with the lives of other persons
around them.

Emotional disturbances can occur at any stage of life, and some
specific life problems become too much for any of us. We all can
recall times when we have withdrawn from situations, lashed out at

others, escaped into fantasy, or imagined various paranoid possibilities about our bosses or coworkers. Some children seem to
become "stuck" in behavior patterns which, while clearly inappropriate to those around them, have some reward for the
children.

Because there is some confusion about emotional disturbances or
mental illness and mental retardation, the following distinctions
should be considered.

MENTAL RETARDATION.   Mental retardation refers to subaverage intellectual functioning. Retardation usually occurs during
the period of development or is present at birth, although a brain
injury or toxemia may cause retardation in anyone at any age. In
mental retardation the intellectual impairment is permanent but
can be compensated through development of the person's potential.
A retarded person can usually be expected to behave rationally at
his operational level, and will not be violent except in those
situations that cause violence in nonretarded persons. A mentally
retarded person has a learning disability and uses the skills of
educators, psychologists, and vocational rehabilitation technicians.

MENTAL ILLNESS. A mentally ill person may be very competent
socially but have a character disorder or other aberrations. Mental
illness can strike at any time. Mental illness is often temporary and
in most cases is reversible. It is not a developmental disability. A
mentally ill person may vacillate between normal and irrational
behavior, and may be erratic or even violent. A mentally ill person
utilizes the services of psychiatrists, physicians, and so on.[3]

The child who is emotionally handicapped has difficulties with
learning which cannot be traced to intellectual, sensory or health
causes, as well as a frequent inability to create and maintain
interpersonal relations. Some signs of such a disability include:
inappropriate or immature feelings and behavior in normal circumstances; excessive behavior including hyperactivity, aggressive
behavior, or depression and withdrawal; and a pattern of developing physical problems, pains, or fears often unrealistically associated with personal problems, other children, or adults in the

environment. The child's behavioral excesses often create learning difficulties. However, not all children who have "unacceptable" behavior are emotionally handicapped. Most unacceptable behavior will occasionally be displayed by "normal" children. It is the consistency of such behavior over time which should concern the media specialist or teacher.

The media specialist can assist the emotionally handicapped child in several ways. First, the environment of the center which the media specialist and staff create impacts all students. A carefully planned approach to activities and to excessive emotional displays helps. Media center staff members need to discuss and develop a consistent approach to specific problems so that the child "bouncing from one to another" will experience a structure which cannot be manipulated. Consistent praise for appropriate behavior of the emotionally handicapped student and of other students is also helpful. A part of the media center environment may need to be a "safe" place where children can be by themselves by choice, or be placed when behavior becomes disruptive. William I. Gardner and R. Vance Hall both present strategies for encouraging acceptable behavior and ignoring or isolating negative behavior which are helpful in designing programs to assist acceptable behavior development. A media center staff that can recognize a child's feelings and respond in a sensitive, flexible way is a real asset. They serve as a model for appropriate behavior by not overreacting, by being firm, by encouraging student initiative, by providing options so that students are not "trapped" into repetitions of behavior, but have acceptable alternatives. Jack Canfield and Harold C. Wells suggest that these children need assistance in developing their self-concepts and concepts of others. Barbara H. Baskin and Karen H. Harris point out that emotionally handicapped students need more physical space than other children and can very easily feel crowded or cornered.

Second, media center programs and activities can contribute to the process of managing emotional handicaps. If the environment and staff of the media center is considered "safe," the child may actively participate in story hour dramas, or may participate from a hidden location—thereby trying on models of appropriate ways of expressing feelings. Games, microcomputers, or programmed instructional devices may be used by children who are not yet ready to deal with groups of peers or participate in group activities.

In managing the media center rules should be kept simple and clear and should be very specific about what is considered appropriate behavior. "Be quiet," "act like good children," or "don't disturb people" are *not* good examples. Programs and activities should be reinforced by repetition, by visuals, by signs. Structured programs should be brief enough to keep the students' interest and allow for children to "drop out" at various points into alternative activities of interest to them.

Third, programs and activities need careful analysis in terms of the level of activities. Active games or programs may build up tensions. Competitive activities should be placed with individual or cooperative activities. The program should allow for quiet activities. Media center activities should allow for varied levels of ability so that students are not consistently frustrated by failure. When a problem seems to be brewing, moving next to the child or establishing physical contact may be helpful in redirecting his or her energy.

Finally, the potential good media center resources can do should not be underestimated. We can all recall a time when some particular song, poem, book, or painting made a profound impact at a critical point in our lives. Media center personnel who can recapture such moments or help children find and share such moments have a powerful tool. This suggestion should not be taken to mean that media specialists become trained bibliotherapists or registered poetry or art therapists. Simply put, a love of good media can be communicated.

Notes

1. Leopold D. Lippman, *Attitudes Toward the Handicapped*, p. 9.

2. National Advisory Committee on Handicapped Children, *Better Education for Handicapped Children*, p. 27.

3. Adapted from Dolores Hurley, "Recognizing and Handling the Mentally Retarded," Lesson Plan—Florida Association for Retarded Citizens, Tallahassee, Fla., 1972.

References

Aiello, Barbara. *Making It Work: Practical Ideas for Integrating Exceptional Children in Regular Classrooms*. Reston, Va.: Council for Exceptional Children, 1975.

Aylor, Kay E. "Seeing Better with Blindfolds." *American Education* 8 (May 1972): 35.

Banes, E. *Children Learn Together: The Integration of Handicapped Children Into Schools*. Syracuse: Human Policy Press, 1974. (Now available on a slide/tape, 1978.)

Barton, S. "The Educational Environment: Mainstreaming the Hard-of-Hearing Child." In *Our Forgotten Children: Hard-of-Hearing Pupils in the Schools*, ed. J. Davis. Minneapolis: University of Minnesota, 1977, pp. 19-24.

Baskin, Barbara H., and Harris, Karen H. *Notes from a Different Drummer: A Guide to Juvenile Fiction Portraying the Handicapped*. New York: Bowker, 1977.

Bender, Michael, and Valletutti, Peter J. *Teaching the Moderately and Severely Handicapped: Curriculum Objectives, Strategies, and Activities*. 4 vols. Baltimore: University Park Press, 1976.

Biklen, Douglas, and Bagdan, R. *Handicapism*. Syracuse: Human Policy Press, 1978. (131 slides and tapes.)

Billings, Mary Dewitt. *Coping: Books About Young People Surviving Special Problems*. Washington, D.C.: Government Printing Office, 1977.

Bisshop, Patricia. *Books About Handicaps: For Children and Young Adults*. East Providence, Rhode Island: Meeting House School, Rhode Island Easter Seal Society, 1978.

Brown, W. P.; Vanderheiden, G. C.; and Harris, D. *1977 Bibliography on Non-Vocal Communication Techniques and Aids*. Madison, Wis.: Trace Research and Development Center for Severely Communicatively Handicapped, 1977.

Canfield, Jack, and Wells, Harold C. *100 Ways to Enhance Self-Concept in the Classroom*. Englewood Cliffs, N.J.: Prentice-Hall, 1976.

Corn, Anne L., and Martinez, Iris. *When You Have a Visually Handicapped Child in Your Classroom*. New York: American Foundation for the Blind, 1977.

Davis, J. *Our Forgotten Children: Hard-of Hearing Pupils in the Schools*. Minneapolis: Audiovisual Library Service, University of Minnesota, 1977.

Di Carlo, Louis M. "Speech, Language, and Cognitive Abilities of the Hard-of-Hearing." *Proceedings of the Institute on Aural Rehabilitation*, University of Denver, 1968.

Dresang, Eliza T. "There Are No *Other* Children." *School Library Journal* 24 (September 1977): 19-23.

Dreyer, Sharon Spredemann. *The Bookfinder: A Guide to Children's Literature About the Needs and Problems of Youth Aged 2-15.* New York: American Guidance Service, 1977.

Edgington, Dorothy. *The Physically Handicapped Child in Your Classroom.* Springfield, Ill: Charles C. Thomas, 1976.

Everson, Robert, and Brady, James. *Mental Retardation: Clearing Away Some of the Smoke.* Spring City, Pa.: Pinehurst State School, 1975.

Fairchild, Thomas N. *Mainstreaming Exceptional Children.* 6 vols. Austin, Tex.: Learning Concepts, 1976.

Fine, Peter J. *Deafness in Infancy and Early Childhood.* New York: Medcom Press, 1974.

Gardner, William I. *Behavior Modification: An Approach to Education of Young Children with Learning and Behavior Difficulties.* Chicago: National Easter Seal Society for Crippled Children and Adults, 1975.

Gold, Marc. "Research in the Vocational Habilitation of the Retarded: the Present, the Future." In *International Review of Research in Mental Retardation,* vol. 6, ed. Norman R. Ellis. New York: Academic Press, 1973.

Grzynkowicz, Wineva. *Meeting the Needs of Learning Disabled Children in the Regular Class.* Springfield, Ill.: Charles C. Thomas, 1974.

Hagemeyer, Alice. "Special Needs of the Deaf Patron." In *Serving Physically Disabled People: An Information Handbook for All Libraries,* ed. Ruth A. Velleman. New York: Bowker, 1979, pp. 140-61.

Hall, R. Vance. *Managing Behavior Series.* Lawrence, Kans.: H. & H. Enterprises, 1971-1972.

Hanninen, Kenneth A. *Teaching the Visually Handicapped.* Columbus, Ohio: Charles E. Merrill, 1975.

Hatlen, P. H. "Priorities in Education Programs for Visually Handicapped Children and Youth." *Division for the Visually Handicapped Newsletter* 20 (Winter 1976): 8-11.

Hobbs, Nicholas, et al. *Issues in the Classification of Children: A Sourcebook on Categories, Labels, and Their Consequences.* San Francisco: Jossey-Bass, 1975.

Interracial Books for Children Bulletin 8 (1977), nos. 6, 7. (Special double issue on handicapism.)

Katz, Lee; Mathis, S. L.; and Merrill, E. C. *The Deaf Child in the Public Schools: A Handbook for Parents.* Danville, Ill.: Interstate, 1974.

Kennedy, Patricia, and Bruininks, Robert H. "Social Status of Hearing Impaired Children in Regular Classrooms." *Exceptional Children* 40 (February 1974): 336-42.

72   Kieth C. Wright

Kirk, Samuel A., and Gallagher, James J. *Educating Exceptional Children.* Boston: Houghton Mifflin Co., 1972.

Koch, Richard, and Koch, K. *Understanding the Mentally Retarded Child: A New Approach.* New York: Random House, 1974.

Kriegal, Leonard. "Uncle Tom and Tiny Tim: Some Reflections on the Cripple as Negro." *American Scholar* 83 (Summer 1969): 413-14.

Lippman, Leopold D. *Attitudes Toward the Handicapped: A Comparison between Europe and the United States.* Springfield, Ill.: Charles C. Thomas, 1972.

Lloyd, L. *Communication Assessment and Intervention Strategies.* Baltimore: University Park Press, 1976.

Lott, L. A.; Hvdak, B. J.; and Schutz, J. *Strategies and Techniques for Mainstreaming: A Resource Room Handbook.* Monroe County (Michigan) Intermediate School District, 1975.

McDonald, S., and Parnell, D. *The Blind Student in the Regular Classroom: A Guide for Teachers and Students.* Victoria, B.C.: Government of British Columbia, Department of Education, 1976.

McIntyre, R., and Engel, R. C. "Some Neglected Criteria in the Selection for Mentally Retarded Pupils." *Teaching Exceptional Children* 2 (Fall 1969): 13-18.

Metsker, C., and King, E. W. *Hints and Activities for Mainstreaming.* Dansville, N.Y.: Instructor Publications, 1977.

Milner, M. *Breaking Through the Deafness Barrier: Environmental Accommodations for Hearing Impaired People.* Washington, D.C.: Gallaudet College Physical Plant, n.d.

Mindell, Eugene, and Vernon, McCoy. *They Grow in Silence.* Silver Springs, Md.: National Association of the Deaf, 1971.

Moore, Coralie B., and Morton, Kathryn G. *A Readers's Guide for Parents of Children with Mental, Physical, or Emotional Disabilities.* Washington, D.C.: Government Printing Office, 1976.

Mullins, June, and Wolf, Suzanne. *Special People Behind the Eight Ball.* Johnstown, Pa.: Mafax Associates, 1977.

Napier, C. D.; Kappan, D. L.; Tuttle, D.; Schrothberger, W. L.; and Dennison, A. *Handbook for Teachers of the Visually Handicapped.* Louisville, Ky: American Printing House for the Blind, 1974.

National Advisory Committee on Handicapped Children. *Better Education for Handicapped Children.* 2d annual report. Washington, D.C.: Department of Health, Education, and Welfare, 1969.

National Center on Educational Media and Materials for the Handicapped. *Standard Criteria for the Selection and Evaluation of Instructional Material.* ERIC Document Reproduction Service, ED 132 760, 1976.

National Library Service for the Blind and Physically Handicapped. *Reading, Writing, and Other Communication Aids for Visually and Physically Handicapped Persons.* Washington, D.C.: Service Reference Department, 1978.

Noahes, Edward. "Making Libraries Usable." *Wilson Library Bulletin* 40 (May 1966): 851-53.

Orlansky, J. Z. *Mainstreaming the Hearing Impaired Child: An Educational Alternative.* Boston: Teaching Resource Corp., 1977.

Orlansky, Michael D. *Mainstreaming the Visually Impaired Child.* Austin, Tex.: Learning Concepts, 1977.

Project RUN. *Bibliography of Resources for Serving the Handicapped.* Oxford: North Mississippi Retardation Center, 1978.

Putnam, Lee. "Information Needs of Hearing Impaired People." *HRLSD Journal* 2 (1976).

Reynolds, Lyle G. "The School Adjustment of Children with Minimal Hearing Loss." *Journal of Speech and Hearing Disorders* 20 (1955): 380-84.

Ross, M. "Classroom Acoustics and Speech Intelligibility." In *Handbook of Clinical Audiology,* ed. Jack Katz. Baltimore: Williams and Wilkins, 1972.

Sale, R. T. *Economic Concerns: Summary and Issues on Employment of the Handicapped.* Washington, D.C.: White House Conference on Handicapped Individuals, 1975.

Schlesinger, Hilde S., and Meadow, Kathryn P. *Sound and Sigh: Childhood Deafness and Mental Health.* Berkeley: University of California Press, 1973.

Scott, E. *The Partially Sighted Student in School: A Guide for Teachers.* Toronto: Canadian National Institute for the Blind, 1976.

Scott, Robert A. *The Making of Blind Men.* New York: Russell Sage Foundation, 1969.

Selvin, Hanan C. "The Librarian and the Blind Patron." In *Serving Physically Disabled People: An Information Handbook for All Libraries,* ed. Ruth A. Velleman. New York: Bowker, 1979.

Serving Hard of Hearing Pupils: Alternative Strategies for Personal Preparation. Minneapolis: Leadership Training Institute/Special Education, University of Minnesota, 1978.

Spearman, C. *Methods, Techniques, and Teacher Made Material Activity Project as Part of In-Service Education for Regular Classroom Teachers Working with Mildly or Moderately Handicapped Students.* Lakewood, Colo.: Jefferson County School District R-1, n.d.

ten Broek, Jacob, and Matson, Floyd W. "The Disabled and the Law of Welfare." *California Law Review* 54 (May 1966): 809-40.

Turner, Dorothy B. "Where It All Begins." *Learning Today* 6 (Summer 1973): 89-90.
Velleman, Ruth A. "Library Adaptation for the Handicapped." *Library Journal* 99 (October 15, 1975): 2713-16.
_____. *Serving Physically Disabled People: An Information Handbook for All Libraries.* New York: Bowker, 1979.
Wright, Kieth C. *Library and Information Services for Handicapped Individuals.* Littleton, Colo.: Libraries Unlimited, 1979.

4

SELECTING MATERIALS FOR THE MAINSTREAMED LIBRARY

Barbara H. Baskin and Karen H. Harris

Before the enactment of Public Law 94-142, special needs children were routinely, and often exclusively, educated with students who were similarly disabled. Their academic experiences typically focused on remediating or compensating for identified deficiencies. Specially designed or adapted materials and methods were employed that frequently yielded a significantly different school life for these youth. Even when special classes were held in regular schools, the youngsters attending them were perceived as having such particular needs that they could not be accommodated in an unmodified environment. Custom, inertia, lack of knowledge, and sometimes hostility prevented disabled youngsters from participating in such supportive and enriching functions of the school as art and music programs, physical education classes, and library media center activities. As a result of these practices, and the restrictions directly imposed by their impairment, disabled children were exempted from many experiences their peers took for granted.

Under these circumstances, in-school social and recreational encounters were also contingent on the type or severity of the impairment. Consequently, social growth took place within a narrow framework with few opportunities to try out behavior and strategies which could prove successful in unsegregated milieux. On the other hand, nonimpaired children were similarly deprived of the means of learning how to respond appropriately to children needing special consideration. They were unable to discover areas of common interest, ways to be helpful without encouraging dependence, or the means for establishing mutually satisfying friendships.

With the advent of mainstreaming, many of the restrictions imposed on exceptional children were lifted. Children with special needs are now entering school library media centers in increasing numbers. Librarians are called upon to provide support for curricular goals, inculcate a love for learning, introduce reading as a lifelong source of pleasure, and provide materials and model behavior which can ease the transition into a fuller, richer, more varied, rewarding school life.

The Collection

The initial task of any school library is to assemble appropriate materials for those who will be using the collection. Selection to meet the needs of disabled youngsters is guided by the same principle that determines selection for all other populations: choose materials that will satisfy the interests, needs, and abilities of the patrons. The interests of exceptional children are as varied and diverse as those of their age-mates. They experience the same enthusiasms and share the same concerns of their generation, and, like all other children, are unique individuals whose imagination may be captured by any topic from aardvarks to zygotes.

Libraries serving children, impaired or otherwise, should provide print and nonprint materials which address information, developmental, and recreational needs. Readers require information to satisfy their curiosity as well as for school assignments. They should encounter literature that can help them meet the inevitable personal, familial, and social challenges that accompany maturation. And, most of all, they should become convinced that library media centers house books and materials which are inexhaustable sources of pleasure, relaxation, excitement, and understanding.

General Considerations

It is in the area of abilities that exceptional children most differ from their peers and where they are most apt to need special accommodations. Some youngsters may have physical impairments that make the handling of unadapted materials a difficult or even impossible task; others may be limited in their understanding because of intellectual deficits; still others may have problems in receiving or processing information through visual or auditory channels or may find that emotional stress severely limits even a modest level of functioning. With such children, adaptations may have to be made in either the content, format, or presentation of materials if they are to find success and pleasure in their library experiences. For some boys and girls, the content of books and media routinely used by their peers may be too demanding, confusing, or threatening. Other children may be able to deal with intellectually demanding topics, but may have communication disorders which necessitate simplified vocabulary, sentence structure, or the like. Some youngsters may find that print is an unsuitable medium and will have to depend on alternative formats. Youngsters with impaired mobility or difficulty in perceiving, processing, or readily comprehending experiences, or whose behavior in the past caused them to be excluded from various activities, will inevitably lack basic knowledge about their community and culture. These informational gaps often cause confusion and misunderstandings, and care must be taken to identify and fill these lacunae.

Multiple-handicapped children may require adaptations in more than one mode. The possible permutations are virtually unlimited and decisions as to the best responses to their idiosyncratic needs will have to be determined with particular care. Generalizations are particularly hazardous in this area since the degree and variation among children all carrying the same label will be enormous. The type, extent, and specifics of any individual child's impairment will signal what adaptations—if any—are appropriate.

To insure that professionals involved in the education of exceptional children specifically attend to their learning requirements, the law demands that every special needs child must be provided with a specially designed program called an IEP, or Individualized Educational Plan. This prescriptive guide accommodates the particular strengths and weaknesses of each child by providing for the formulation of an agenda of academic action based on her or his educational and health profile. An IEP specifies a timetable and includes the particular techniques and materials to be employed in the achievement of each educational, social, and recreational goal. Selection, then, is a critical aspect of the legally mandated educational activity, and materials used in a library or media center setting should contribute to the support of each child's academic, recreational, and social requirements.

The Context

The considerations to be weighed in the selection process are illustrated in Figure 1. The factors represented by the top circle have primacy over the others for two important reasons: achievement is highest when children are able to work in content areas of specific interest to them, and learning is maximized when youngsters can work through strengths rather than weaknesses.

Disabilities impose constraints on the content and/or the structure of materials which can be used successfully with exceptional youngsters. Although the type, extent, and severity can vary extensively, the reality of impairment generates restrictions in some aspect of functioning. Consequently certain materials will be useless with particular populations and substitutions will have to be made so that these children can work through their most intact or fully functioning modalities.

The format in which information is presented possesses possibilities of successful usage with some youngsters, but provides restrictive impediments for others. Which communication channels are used—visual, auditory, tactile, or some combination—are significant factors to consider. Whether the data can be transmitted in a fully automatic mode, how much interaction between child and materials is required, and whether confirmation and reinforcement are integral components of the materials may all be decisive factors in the selection of appropriate instructional tools for particular users.

FIGURE 1   **Selection Considerations**

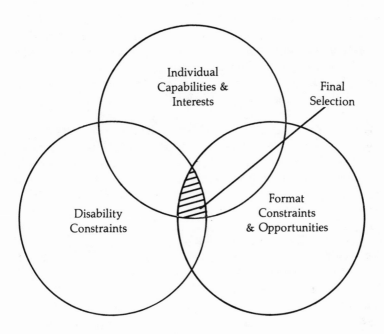

Physical Impairment

The interests of physically handicapped children usually parallel those of their age-mates. Recently there has been much media attention to the participation of disabled persons in activities once thought beyond their capabilities. They are involved in strenuous sports, enter and succeed in demanding occupations, adopt life styles that are exciting, unconventional, even exotic. As children they need books which open these vistas and suggest previously unthought-of possibilities. Even those children who will always be severely limited in activity are able, through books, to vicariously experience a world that for them may never be directly known. They should not be protected from such works because of the misapprehension that such knowledge would be painful.

Generally, then, youth with orthopedic and neurological impairments, as well as those with disabling illnesses that impair motor functioning, need books and media on the same topics as their peers, but may need to have access to additional titles especially selected to address their particular limitations. In recent years, juvenile titles on topics such as cooking, crafts, travel, camping, and so on, have appeared which have been specifically designed for this readership. Additionally, resource books are now available that specify camps, schools, universities, travel services, and the like which provide adapted accommodations in either special or mainstreamed settings. Such volumes should be included in the references of a well-stocked library.

Some books which address such special teenage concerns as peer relationships, dating, sexuality, and so forth, may not be sufficiently useful for this population. Adolescence is a particularly challenging time for these students, and carefully selected titles which are honest and forthright can help them develop a positive, realistic, and self-accepting attitude as they try to reconcile social pressures and expectations with their own emerging identity, capabilities, and goals.

Some few school age youngsters have progressively debilitating terminal disorders and are in particular need of help in coming to terms with their prognosis. They need assistance in maximizing their intact abilities and partaking of those pleasures life has to offer for as long as they are able. Selecting materials and contexts that emphasize normalizing aspects of their situation is of critical importance.

Most physically disabled children will need few other special adaptations in the content of the collection. If the environment is barrier free, they will, for the most part, choose and use the same materials as their peers. Some, however, will need special formats. The Library of Congress has made talking book services available to anyone who cannot handle standard print well. Some children with muscular, skeletal, or neurological disorders or those handicapped by chronic health problems have found hours of pleasure through this resource. Some few readers will be able to handle paperback editions more easily than hardbound ones although others may adequately manage the latter with the assistance of mechanical page turners.

Intellectual Impairment

The interests of retarded children are similar to, but more restricted than, those of their peers. These youngsters often lack the skill to initiate and sustain interpersonal relationships, a problem which may distress them far more than academic failure would, and so they need books and materials which can foster social skills and provide good models.

Their more obvious deficit, however, is in the area of intellectual functioning. Typically, these students are inefficient learners: language skills are inadequately developed; attention and concentration span is limited; they are generally only able to focus on one topic at a time and cannot deal easily with several ideas simultaneously; they are less able than their age-mates to separate the main idea from peripheral or extraneous issues; they often have extensive gaps in their knowledge base; and they deal best with concrete, specific, experience-derived ideas rather than abstract, generalized, or theoretical concepts.

As a consequence of their limitations, these girls and boys need highly attractive material which incorporates considerable redundancy and reinforcement if learning is to take place. It is imperative that text and illustrations in books be consistent and free of discrepancies and that stories not have distracting minor or parallel plots, shifting narrators or points of view, or extraneous elements added for "color." Each story should have unity of plot and theme and should develop through a step-by-step, logical or chronological progression. These youngsters need materials which are identical in appearance to those used by peers, for they will reject books or media they perceive as stigmatizing or babyish. They do not need materials which are ambiguous, paradoxical, ironic, or lacking in closure since these qualities tend to be confusing and frustrating rather than challenging. Many of these students may benefit from multisensory experiences such as those found in combined media approaches. Reading a book while simultaneously hearing the text read on a tape or a record can be an effective and pleasurable learning encounter. Young intellectually impaired children need materials that are of limited length or that can be segmented into brief, self-contained components. They need those materials that address the gaps in their basic knowledge of their immediate environment, thus helping them in the often difficult process of acculturation. In addition to the numerous regular trade titles that satisfy these requirements, many publishers have added high interest/low ability titles to their lists.

Media are frequently recommended for viewers with cognitive or processing problems. When selection of audiovisual materials is made, the following attributes should be considered: instructions or directions which are specific, clearly stated, and in proper sequence with no omissions; slow, clear narration using vocabulary within the expected comprehension level of these patrons; minimal use of metaphorical or nonliteral language; a single, clear, overly stated theme; absence of any diversionary information, digressions, or distracting components; a slow, clear, and repetitive presentation which includes a summary of key elements; and content, visual images, and language which are age appropriate.

Special attention should be paid to the virtues of serials as a major resource for mentally retarded youth. Many popular magazines contain brief, generously illustrated articles with features written in a direct, well-paced style, containing a vocabulary within the reach of these youngsters. In some, captioned pictures carry enough of the message so that the ideas can be understood even if portions of the text are incomprehensible. Such magazines act to camouflage the discrepancy between intellectually impaired children and their age-mates, often providing bridges for sharing interests with their own nonimpaired contemporaries. Periodicals, although directed to the general public, can be used successfully by this population, and are the materials most apt to spark a lifetime reading habit.

Visual Impairment

Visually impaired children may have the same range of interests and abilities as those without this sensory deficit. Because they live in a world in which overwhelming amounts of information are obtained through the visual channels, they must learn to use efficiently what sight they may still have. In some instances when residual vision is low or absent, they will need to rely on tactile and auditory channels for supplementation or substitution. Format then is the critical variable in choosing materials for blind or low vision children. With judicious selection policies and procedures, there is no reason why these youngsters should experience reduced access to the literary world.

Many picture books are designed with print size of eighteen point, twenty point, or larger type and contain pictures which are large, clear, and uncluttered, and characterized by good color contrasts where the print is not superimposed over distracting illustrations. For older children, large print books, now available in covers which make them similar in external appearance to standard books, facilitate ready access to literature. Some girls and boys may benefit from portable magnifiers to make small or unclear images more discernible. Realia has always been a particularly effective supplement for these children. Tactile differentiation in surface qualities and scale reduction without loss or inclusion of critical attributes are important considerations.

For those who depend on tactile or auditory channels, there are two relatively recent, highly significant technological advances. One is the Optacon, which uses a miniature camera to scan standard print, then translates the images into tactile messages. The compactness, limited weight, and hence, easy portability of this device makes it highly desirable, particularly in promoting access

to newspapers, monthly journals, some foreign language newspapers, and other topical reading matter. Although there are still
some minor problems to be resolved, the Kurzweil machine can
read standard print-type copy, computer printout, books, journals,
and so on, and convey the source document as an audible message.
In other words, the Kurzweil acts as an electronic friend who
accepts any printed word and reads it aloud to a blind listener.
Talking books as well as brailled materials are provided free by the
National Library Service for the Blind and Physically Handicapped
of the Library of Congress. Selection and utilization of these
materials are facilitated by the provision of comprehensive subject
catalogs and free loan and maintenance of record and tape players.
All these possibilities are important options for patrons who cannot
rely on vision for information gathering. Selection will depend
both on the resources available and the needs and preferences of the
user.

One special type of material has particular significance in promoting mainstreaming goals: Twin Vision Books contain both
standard print and braille in the same volume. These allow blind
and sighted children to share an experience in which both can read
simultaneously, each in the appropriate mode.

Hearing Impairment

Severe hearing loss at birth or in early childhood places an
enormous learning burden on youngsters. Even with early intervention, most of these children experience communication difficulties that seriously impede language development. This generally results in reading levels below what their intellectual abilities
would otherwise presumably have permitted. Because the process
of concept and vocabulary acquisition is so arduous, and because
the subtleties involved in more complex grammatical construction
are so elusive, high interest/low ability books, originally developed
for other populations, are often equally useful for these youngsters.

Educators who work with children sustaining auditory deficits
are heavily dependent on technology to assist in the instructional
process. In addition to such specially designed materials as Captioned Films for the Deaf, nonnarrated 16 mm films, captioned

filmstrips, 8 mm loops, models, realia, games, and programmed materials can transmit information otherwise relayed through the voice. Overhead projection is a particularly valuable procedure for the integrated deaf student since eye contact can be maintained and reflected light from the stage illuminates the speaker's face, thus facilitating speechreading. Signing can also be used during projection since it is not necessary to darken the room for this medium.

Learning Disabilities

The term "learning disabilities" covers such a range and diversity of impairments that it is difficult to make generalizations about children so described. The expression encompasses anyone who has serious difficulty in receiving, interpreting, or expressing information transmitted through the senses, even though those organs are undamaged. These children usually have average or above average intellectual abilities and the cause of their diminished functioning is not attributable to problems of visual or auditory acuity. These youth may display, on occasion, such symptoms as hyperactivity, distractability, short attention span, poor memory, and an inability to separate peripheral from core messages. They may be aware of and understand their peer culture, but are often excluded from it because of their poor social skills and behaviors which others tend to regard as annoying, inappropriate, or immature. Too often, a poor-self-concept, caused by social and academic failure, exacerbates their situation.

In selecting materials for learning disabled children, both content and format need to be assessed. Often social ostracism is perceived as a far greater problem than academic failure. Stories which can sensitize them to and help them interpret the interpersonal behavior of others are of particular importance. Since these youngsters typically have trouble in many aspects of organization, books need to be provided which have a single unified theme without subplots, extraneous characters, or other potentially distracting elements. Texts and illustrations should be mutually supportive with the latter depicting all the major characters and the central concerns of the work. In stories, straightforward chronological narratives that maintain a consistent point of view and provide obvious closure are suggested. Pictures should be clear, well outlined, uncluttered, with contrasting colors defining spaces. Pages ideally should have ample leading. For some children, auditory channels should be completely bypassed; for others, visual channels are too inefficient and these boys and girls may do better with the instructional emphasis on audio materials. Special design features involving multisensory learning may intensify the instructional potential of certain formats for some youngsters. Scratch and sniff books should be available for them. Books with narration on accompanying tape or record will be helpful for some, especially if the rate of presentation is properly paced. For other children, however, simultaneous audio and visual input creates sensory overload. These children can profitably look at or listen to stimuli separately but may be uncomfortable with such multisensory materials as sound filmstrips.

Emotional Dysfunction

Children who have emotional disorders may exhibit the same range of intellectual ability as their nonimpaired peers. Their problems frequently interfere with their functioning though, and consequently they too may experience serious problems that interfere with academic success. These youth typically have difficulty attending to and completing a task, are distractable, and may have a poor attention span. Like everyone else they have a high need for success, although in their case it may be much exaggerated. Books which may be too challenging should be avoided initially. In new situations these youngsters may want materials below their abilities so they can be confident of avoiding failure. Later, exposure to titles of superior quality may be useful for children capable of handling more demanding fare.

   Books on threatening topics should be avoided. The enthusiasm for so-called relevance in children's literature has resulted in the publication of numerous works on child abuse, desertion, substance abuse, gang violence, and so on—all of which are likely to be inappropriate for emotionally dysfunctional youth. In terms of content, it is particularly important that materials illustrating models of acceptable coping behavior be offered as well as ones which reinforce societal values.

Children who have experienced extensive failure with print materials may be more comfortable and confident using other media. Two cautions should be noted: the range and focus of phobias is infinite so if children exhibit avoidance behavior in relation to certain formats, their resistance should be respected; contrarily, some youngsters may find media which combine audio and visual messages excessively stimulating and here, too, their preferences should be accommodated. Paperbacks, magazines, and other materials which camouflage poor reading habits and allow those students who are frequently underachievers to blend into the mainstream should be readily available.

Mainstreaming

In addition to choosing books and other materials which respond to the needs of disabled library users, it is imperative that a collection contain works *about* impairments and impaired persons for the enlightenment of nonhandicapped patrons. No matter how much instruction, support, and guidance disabled children receive, if their peers are hostile and rejecting, then mainstreaming will be a sham.

Children have many erroneous ideas about people with disabilities. These are often based on inaccurate information, superstitions, and faulty perceptions. To help correct these distortions, children need books which honestly and forthrightly, without exaggeration or misrepresentation, depict disabled people. Not all titles are accurate, constructive, or empathic: many treat the disabled with pity or condescension, or emphasize helplessness and dependence, thus setting them apart from the rest of humanity. Fortunately, in recent years, a great number of first-rate titles have appeared which meet stringent standards of accuracy and quality of information in tandem with literary excellence.

Children with special needs must have the skills and competencies that allow them to function outside the sheltered, segregated environment in which they have been confined for too long. Equally important, members of the larger community must be readied to receive those once excluded. Libraries, and their selection policies, have a critical role to play in answering the needs of both these populations if mainstreaming is to become a viable social reality.

References

Banbury, Mary M. "Remediation and Reinforcement: Books for Children
with Visual and Perceptual Impairments." *Top of the News* 37 (Fall
1980): 40-46.

Baskin, Barbara H., and Harris, Karen H. *Notes from a Different Drummer: A Guide to Juvenile Fiction Portraying the Handicapped*. New
York: Bowker, 1977.

————. *The Special Child in the Library*. Chicago: American Library
Association, 1976.

Bush, Margaret. "Books for Children Who Cannot See the Printed Page."
School Library Journal 26 (April 1980): 28-31.

Cohen, Sandra B.; Alberto, Paul A.; and Troutman, Ann. "Selecting and
Developing Educational Materials: An Inquiry Approach." *Teaching Exceptional Children* 12 (Fall 1979): 7-11.

Forer, Ann-Marie, and Zojoc, Mary. "Library Services to the Mentally
Retarded." Bethesda: ERIC Document Reproduction Service, ED
165 728, 1979.

Kirk, Samuel A. *Educating Exceptional Children*. 2d ed. Boston: Houghton
Mifflin Co., 1972.

Velleman, Ruth A. *Serving Physically Disabled People: An Information
Handbook for All Libraries*. New York: Bowker, 1979.

5

DEVELOPING AND IMPLEMENTING AN INDIVIDUALIZED EDUCATIONAL PROGRAM FOR THE HANDICAPPED CHILD

Ellen C. Fagan

In these days it is doubtful that any child may reasonably be expected to succeed in life if he is denied the opportunity to an education. Such an opportunity, where the state has undertaken to provide it, is a right which must be made available to all on equal terms.[1]

Due Process and Public Law 94-142

The largest single institution in America today is the public school system. Inside these learning facilities are children from a varied range of educational, cultural, and social environments. Intellectually gifted, mulatto, and ghetto street children may all be placed in the same classroom setting. However, regardless of the varied backgrounds from which these children come, the school system must meet their educational needs.

Prior to 1975, few people believed that handicapped children could benefit from education. They assumed that handicapped persons represented a disadvantaged minority who competed ineffectually for education, employment, and many other basic necessities in society. In 1975 Congress conducted a study and found that more than half of this nation's eight million handicapped children were not receiving appropriate educational services.

It was not until the latter part of the 1960s that advances were made regarding the educational opportunities of handicapped individuals. Legal proceedings were initiated, seeking to improve these opportunities. Perhaps the principal lawsuits that laid the groundwork in this area of educating all individuals, including the handicapped, were *Pennsylvania Association for Retarded Children* v. *Commonwealth of Pennsylvania*, in which the right to a free appropriate education for mentally retarded children was upheld, and *Mills* v. *Board of Education of the District of Columbia*, in which the federal district court concluded that all handicapped children have a right to education, even where funds available for education are limited. As a result of these and similar decisions, by 1974 the question was no longer whether handicapped children had a right to education, but rather how their education could be implemented and funded.

In November 1975, Congress passed Public Law 94-142 and the Education of All Handicapped Children Act. This act provides that each handicapped child must have a specially planned individualized educational program (IEP). The IEP is the central element behind Public Law 94-142. An IEP outlines, in writing, the educational and supportive services which will be provided for each student who requires special education. The following information must be included in each child's individual education plan: (1) a statement of the child's present levels of educational performance, (2) a statement of annual goals including short-term instructional objectives, (3) a statement of the specific education and related services to be provided to the child, and the extent to which the child will be able to participate in regular educational programs, (4) projected dates of initiation of services and anticipated duration of the services, and (5) appropriate objectives, evaluation procedures, and schedules for determining on at least an annual basis whether the short-term instructional objectives are being achieved.

It is not the intent of this law to draw attention to or ridicule those students placed in special programs. However, the crucial issue, which is the core to providing an appropriate individualized education, is the placement of the handicapped student in the "least restrictive environment." By "least restrictive environment," the law insures that handicapped children are educated with children who are not handicapped, and that special classes, separate schooling, and other removal of handicapped children from the regular education environment occurs only when the nature or severity of the handicap is such that education in regular classes with the use of supplementary aids and services cannot be achieved satisfactorily.

Under Public Law 94-142, regular class placement is thought to be least restrictive because the student can receive an appropriate individualized education at the least distance from the mainstream of regular education. Patricia Motz feels that it is not only an advantage for a retarded or handicapped person to be normalized or mainstreamed with peers in a public school setting, but perhaps even a greater gift for the "normal" individual to be with a person who cannot walk or talk, or needs to be fed. This exposure helps the "normal" person to appreciate just what good health really means.

According to Sy Du Bow, a legal director for the National Center for Law and the Deaf at Gallaudet College in Washington, D.C., "one of the best features of the Education for All Handicapped Children Act is the procedural safeguards guaranteed to handicapped children and their parents."[2] This act requires school systems to inform parents of their rights and to provide notice regarding their child's evaluation and placement. Parents are required to submit written consent for testing and special education placement, and to approve or disapprove their child's IEP. Written notice must be provided to the parents every time an agency proposes to initiate a change or refuses to initiate a change in the identification or educational placement of the child, or the provision of a free appropriate public education to the child. This notice must also include a detailed account of all procedural safeguards and a description and explanation of action proposed or refused by the agency, and descriptions of any options the agency considered and the reasons why those options were rejected. Also contained within the parental notice is a description of every evaluation procedure, test, record, or report on which the agency based its proposal, and description of any other factors relevant to the agency's proposal or refusal. Public Law 94-142 requires that parents be contacted by way of a letter written in a language used by the parent unless it is impossible to do so (braille, foreign language). If they voice any complaint with respect to any matter relating to the identification, evaluation, or educational placement of the child, or the provision of a free appropriate public education to their child, a due process hearing evolves.

If the parents question the placement of their child, they have the right to request a subsequent evaluation. At this time, it is often to the parents' advantage to seek out a skilled "witness" to evaluate and testify on the school's plan for their child. This third-party participant's intention is to prove that the school's IEP is inappropriate for the child in question.

Under regulations mandated by Public Law 94-142, an impartial hearing officer is required to take part in the proceedings. The hearing officer's duties are to assure procedural fairness during the hearing, hear all the evidence introduced, and make a final decision on the placement of the child. The officer's decision must be based solely on evidence and testing in the record. Decisions made by the hearing officer are final and must be obeyed by the school district and parents, subject only to appeal to the state education agency or the courts.

Although states vary slightly in the procedures utilized within their geographical area, the majority of the due process procedures indicate that, as a minimum: a parent or public education agency can initiate a due process hearing whenever there is a disagreement on the identification, evaluation, placement, or provision of a free appropriate education for a handicapped child; the initial hearing must be held by an impartial hearing officer at the local level; if there is disagreement after the decision of the local hearing officer, an appeal can be made to the state education agency; and, following the decision made at the state level, any party aggrieved by the findings may initiate civil action.

Due process decisions are based on facts presented by both parties involved in a specific case, and on the evaluation laws, rules, and regulations for an individual state. Because decisions are rendered differently according to the state involved, it cannot be thought that similar cases will result in the same decisions in neighboring states. Following is a summary of an appeal hearing conducted in Connecticut.

Parents of a child with a severe language disorder requested a hearing to contest the school district's refusal to pay for the child's academic summer program. The child's IEP, which called for full-time special education, contained no mention of any summer program, but the district had volunteered to pay for a largely recreational summer session. The district's policy on summer programs was that they would be provided when required. The parents argued that the child needed to attend the summer session sponsored by the school which he attended during the regular year. The parents had paid for the child's paticipation in this program in earlier years.

The state hearing officer ruled for the parents, finding that the child required a "full-time special education program." The child's educational progress, the officer concluded, would be irreparably diminished, and serious regression and educational harm would result without a summer program.

Comments: Decisions such as this have been rendered in a number of states, e.g. Massachusetts, Michigan, and Pennsylvania. Consideration of the necessity for an extended year program is made based on the needs of an individual child. If evidence can be provided showing that regression will occur if the child is not enrolled in a summer program, then the LEA (Local Education Agency) may be responsible for providing services for more than the usual 180-day school year.[3]

The following case summary stresses the importance of mainstreaming factual information and instructional gains:

The Committee on the Handicapped (COH) placed a child with a severe hearing impairment in the regular first grade class and provided the child with related services. On the basis of the evaluation during the previous year in kindergarten, the COH determined related services should include individualized instruction, and auditory and speech-reading training, but not a sign language interpreter. After the hearing which affirmed the COH's decisions, the parents appealed, requesting that the child be provided with "total communication" instruction, which combines sign language, finger spelling and audible speech. The parents submitted documents supporting the concept of total communication. The Commisioners of Education dismissed the appeal, ruling that the parents' documents did not address the specific child, and that the record of the child's progress demonstrated appropriateness of the evaluation and placement.

Comments: In this case, the parents were unable to show that the child's placement in the regular classroom using an "oral" approach to instruction was inappropriate. The parents submitted documents from experts supporting the need for a total communication program. The school district documented that the child was progressing satisfactorily in the regular class without a sign language interpreter. The Commissioner indicated that although the documents submitted were informative, they did not relate to the specific child in question. One of the experts had seen the child. Because the school was able to document the child's progress and the parents could not document the lack of progress, the appeal was dismissed.[4]

A major issue at the hearing is whether the proposed placement is appropriate in meeting the educational needs of the handicapped child. The parents of such a child have the following rights at the hearing: (1) the right to counsel and experts in educating handicapped children, (2) the right to present evidence and confront and cross-examine witnesses, (3) the right to obtain a written or electronic verbatim record of the hearing, which is important in an appeal, and the right to have the child remain in its present educational placement unless the school and parents agree otherwise.

In summary, Public Law 94-142 will have wide-ranging effects on education, on state and city programs for children in other sectors, and on the ways in which citizens and professionals view handicapped children. Parents must be fully knowledgeable of their due process rights mandated by the law, in order that the hearing procedures initiated can be an influential check on inappropriate placement.

The Total Service Plan

As previously stated, at the center of Public Law 94-142, the Education of All Handicapped Children Act, is the IEP. The IEP consists of two parts: the Total Service Plan (TSP) and the Individualized Instructional Plan (IIP). The program is individualized because it takes into account the strengths and weaknesses of one individual student. An IEP must be written for each student requiring special educational services. Each handicapped student is assured a free and appropriate education through the IEP; however, the IEP serves several other purposes also. It serves to increase the effectiveness of instruction, provide for better communication among teachers and other professionals, and thus helps to assure greater success for handicapped students. The IEP is carefully monitored and evaluated to assure continued progress. Public Law 94-142 requires that an individualized education program be established or revised for each handicapped child at the beginning of each school year and reviewed periodically, but not less than annually.

The IEP concept of individualized instruction requires teachers to explain in writing the many details of their educational plans. Among other things, they must outline and describe in detail what will be taught and by whom, where the instruction will take place, and for how long. These plans must be measurable and be designed by a group of individuals, many of whom are specialists.

According to the provisions of Public Law 94-142, the child is to be evaluated by a placement committee or a Child Study Team (CST). Depending on the type and extent of the handicap, a CST would include some of the following professionals: regular and special education teachers, vision and hearing specialists, school psychologist, communication disorders specialist, physician, social worker, art and music therapists, and the school media specialist. Following the evaluation, the CST holds a planning meeting to develop an appropriate IEP and to determine where the child should be educated and by whom instruction will be carried out.

All team members should participate in the placement and IEP planning meeting to develop the Total Service Plan. The Total Service Plan gives an overall picture of how the special needs of the student will be met. The team members present at this meeting may include: (1) the child's teacher(s), (2) a representative of the local school district, (3) the child's parent(s), (4) the child (when appropriate), (5) an individual who is knowledgeable about the procedures used to evaluate the child and the results of that evaluation, and (6) other individuals invited by the parents or school district. Often the resource teacher serves as the coordinator or chairperson for the development and completion of the IEP—both the Total Service Plan and the Individualized Instructional Plan.

Criteria must be established to guide decisions about the inclusion or exclusion of the child in the meeting to develop the IEP. Several factors to consider are the student's age and grade level, parental requests, and the student's request.

The parents should be willing to participate and be involved in their child's placement and educational program. They can provide valuable firsthand knowledge of their child which could not be obtained from anyone else. It is important that the parents develop an understanding of the social, emotional, and educational problems facing their child.

The administrator on the IEP team, or a representative of the local educational agency, is there to facilitate the team process during the planning meeting, to insure that an appropriate IEP is developed, and to make certain that due process procedures are followed. The regular classroom teacher is responsible for recognizing the child who is functioning differently from the other children in the class and for determining if the student needs help from other professionals. Although not responsible for diagnosis, the classroom teacher is responsible for referring students with learning problems and for making recommendations at the placement meeting. The teacher also must work with the resource teacher and other team members in implementing the IEP.

The resource teacher serves as diagnostician, instructional specialist, evaluator, team member, and consultant. As a team member, the resource teacher coordinates the development, writing, and revision of the IEP and coordinates the implementation of the Total Service Plan with the help and cooperation of the regular classroom teacher.

The school psychologist administers diagnostic tests and may diagnose the handicapping condition of the student. Also, the school psychologist collects and analyzes information regarding the student's personal-social skills, academic aptitude, adaptive behavior, educational readiness, academic achievement, sensory and perceptual motor functioning, and environmental/cultural influences. The psychologist also participates in the planning meeting by interpreting test results and reporting on other facts gathered.

Support personnel include professionals such as speech-language pathologists, physical therapists, school nurses, doctors, occupational and vocational therapists and counselors, guidance counselors, physical educators, art therapists, music therapists, school media specialists, shop teachers, and so on. These professional's participate as team members based on the needs of the individual student. It is extremely important that each team member work closely with other members in planning the student's Total Service Plan.

In order to meet the requirements of Public Law 94-142, the following components must be included in the IEP Total Service Plan developed for each handicapped child requiring special education and related services: (1) a statement of the child's present levels of educational performance including academic achievement, social adaption, prevocational and vocational skills, psychomotor skills, and self-help skills; (2) a statement of annual goals that describe the educational performance to be achieved by the end of the school year (included in the child's individual education program); (3) a statement of specific educational services needed by the child, with a description of all special educational and related services necessary to meet the unique needs of the child, including the type of physical education program in which the child will participate; (4) the date services will begin and the length of time the services will be given; (5) a description of the extent to which the child will participate in regular education programs; (6) a justification for the type of educational placement that the child will have; (7) a list of the individuals who are responsible for the implementation of the Total Service Plan; and (8) objective criteria, evaluation procedures, and schedules for determining on at least an annual basis whether the short-term instructional objectives are being achieved.

In order to plan more effectively for the individual needs of each child, the following additional components should also be included in the written Total Service Plan: (1) when appropriate, a statement of the modifications to be made in the child's regular education program so that it will meet the child's needs; (2) a statement of the support services or training which will be provided the regular classroom teacher or the special class teacher, and the method and personnel to be used to provide such services or training; (3) a criterion set, in terms of objectives to be met, for returning the child to the next least restrictive environment; (4) a list of all materials, supplies, and equipment necessary to implement the child's individual education plan; (5) a transportation plan, if the child requires special means of transportation to and from school; and (6) specification of any support services which should be provided to the child's parents in order to meet the individual child's educational needs.

Components of the IEP Total Service Plan

The IEP Total Service Plan consists of some twenty-five components (Figure 2). Items 1-6 are identifying information items including the names of the local education agency (school district) and the school, and student's name, date of birth, age in years and months, and grade level.

Item 7 refers to the special education program model. A placement is suggested for the child based on the evaluation of the CST and their recommendations. According to Public Law 94-142, the child must be placed in the least restrictive educational setting. Some placement options, ranging from least to most restrictive, are as follows: (1) The regular classroom with supportive services allows the child to be assigned to a regular classroom. The special education teacher and/or other personnel assist the regular classroom teacher with advice about methods or materials. In this placement option, the child does not receive direct instruction from the support personnel. (2) The regular class with support instruction also allows the child to remain in the regular classroom. The child does receive some direct instruction in the classroom from a special education teacher or other specialist. (3) In the regular class with resource room instruction, the child remains in the regular classroom, but receives some instruction in another location from a

FIGURE 2   Individualized Educational Program: Total Service Plan

Local Education Agency:
Name and Number _____ (1)
School _____ (2)
Name of Student _____ (3)
Date of Birth (4) Age (5) Grade (6)

Description of Educational Placement Recommendations:

Special Education Program Model (7)	Hrs/Week (8)	Regular Education (9)	Hrs/Week (10)	Legal Category of Exceptionality (for funding purposes only) (11)

Summary of Present Levels of Student Performance:

(12)

Program Goal(s)	Specific Special Education and/or Related Services	Person(s) Responsible For Implementation	Hours Per Week	Starting Date	Projected Ending Date	Annual Review Date (Mo-Yr)	Child Study Team Recommendations: Methods & Materials— (if appropriate)	Evaluation Criteria
(13)	(14)	(15)	(16)	(17)	(18)	(19)	(20)	(21)

Child Study Team Members Present

Signature (22)	Position (23)

Agreement with IEP: Total Service Plan
(Check appropriate space)

Yes ____ (24)   No ____

Date of Child Study Team Meeting: ____ (25)

SOURCE: Adapted by the author from Judy A. Schrag, *Individualized Educational Programming (IEP): A Child Study Team Process.* Hingham, Mass.: Teaching Resources Corp., 1977, p. 25.

specialist. (4) In a separate class, part-time, regular school placement, the child is assigned primarily to a special education classroom, but receives some instruction in a regular classroom. (5) The child spends full time in a special education classroom and is not integrated in a regular class in that school. (6) In the special class, part-time, separate facility placement, the child is assigned to a special class in a separate school on a part-time basis. Usually, all of the children in this facility are handicapped. The child also receives some instruction in a facility which has classes for regular and special students. (7) The child placed in the special class, full-time, separate facility, receives all of his or her education in a school for special children. (8) The child assigned to homebound placement receives an educational program in the home from special teachers or other specialists.

Items 8, 9, 10, and 16 of Figure 2 deal with the amount of time per week that the child spends in special education classes and in the regular classroom. The number of hours and which classes the child will attend with nonhandicapped students must be specified. The Total Service Plan must detail the extent to which a child will participate in regular education programs, as some children will be mainstreamed or integrated in regular classes for only a few activities such as music, art, library, and physical education.

Item 11 of Figure 2, "legal category," requires that the child's classification according to handicap be stated on the Total Service Plan. These legal categories are labels used by state and federal governments to determine funding. There are essentially eleven categories used to classify children with handicapping conditions. These include:

MENTALLY RETARDED or MENTALLY HANDICAPPED: Subaverage general intellectual functioning which originates during the developmental period and is associated with impairment in adaptive behavior. These children may also be classified further into four groups based on IQ: Slow Learner (IQ: 80-90), Educable Mentally Handicapped (EMH) (IQ: 50-55 to 75-79), Trainable Mentally Handicapped (TMH) (IQ: 30-35 to 50-55), and Totally Dependent Mentally Handicapped or Profoundly Mentally Handicapped (PMH) (IQ: below 25-30).

ORTHOPEDICALLY HANDICAPPED (OH) or ORTHOPEDICALLY
IMPAIRED (OI): Severe Orthopedic impairment which adversely
affects a child's educational performance. The classification includes impairments caused by congenital anomaly (clubfoot,
absence of a limb, for example), impairments caused by diseases
such as polio or bone tuberculosis, and impairments from other
causes like cerebral palsy, amputations, and fractures or burns
which cause contractures.

DEAF: A hearing impairment severe enough that the child is so
impaired in processing linguistic information through hearing, with
or without amplification, that educational performance is adversely affected.

HARD OF HEARING (HOH): A hearing impairment, permanent
or fluctuating, which adversely affects a child's educational performance but which is not included under the definition of deaf.

VISUALLY HANDICAPPED (VH): A visual impairment which,
even with correction, adversely affects a child's educational performance. The term includes both partially sighted and blind
children.

DEAF-BLIND (DB): Concomitant hearing and visual impairments,
the combination of which causes such severe communication and
other developmental and educational problems that the child
cannot be accommodated in special education programs solely for
deaf or blind children.

OTHER HEALTH IMPAIRED (OHI): Limited strength, vitality, or
alertness due to chronic or acute health problems such as heart
condition, tuberculosis, rheumatic fever, nephritis, asthma, sickle-
cell anemia, hemophilia, epilepsy, lead poisoning, leukemia, or
diabetes, which adversely affect a child's educational performance.

MULTIHANDICAPPED: Concomitant impairments such as mentally retarded-blind or mentally retarded-orthopedically impaired,
the combination of which causes such severe educational problems

that the child cannot be accommodated in special education programs solely for one of the impairments. The term is not used for deaf-blind children.

SERIOUSLY EMOTIONALLY DISTURBED (ED) or *EMOTIONALLY HANDICAPPED* (EH): A condition exhibiting one or more of the following characteristics over a long period of time and to a marked degree, which adversely affect educational performance: (a) inability to learn which cannot be explained by intellectual, sensory, or health factors; (b) inability to build or maintain satisfactory interpersonal relationships with peers and teachers; (c) inappropriate types of behavior or feelings under normal circumstances; (d) a general pervasive mood of unhappiness or depression; or (e) a tendency to develop physical symptoms or fears associated with personal or school problems. The term includes children who are schizophrenic or autistic. The term does not include children who are socially maladjusted, unless it is determined that they are seriously emotionally disturbed.

SPECIFIC LEARNING DISABILITY (LD): A disorder in one or more of the basic psychological processes involved in understanding or in using language, spoken or written, which may manifest itself in an imperfect ability to listen, think, speak, read, write, spell, or to do mathematical calculations. The term includes such conditions as perceptual handicaps, brain injury, minimal brain dysfunction, dyslexia, and developmental aphasia. The term does not include learning problems which are primarily the result of visual, hearing, or motor handicaps, or mental retardation, or of environmental, cultural, or economic disadvantage.

SPEECH IMPAIRED or *SPEECH-LANGUAGE IMPARIED*: A communication disorder which adversely affects a child's educational performance or social development. A speech impaired child may exhibit one or more of the following disorders: *Articulation disorder* is a failure to master the speech sounds of a language system. This may be characterized by substitutions, omissions, distortions, and/or additions of speech sounds. *Voice or vocal disorder* is a deviation of one or more of the three components of voice (vocal) production: quality, pitch, and loudness. *Stuttering* is a pattern of speaking in which rhythms of speech are disrupted or broken by excessive or inappropriate prolongations and/or repetitions of sounds, syllables, words, or parts of sentences; usually accompanied by struggle and/or avoidance behavior. *Cluttering* refers to a disorder of time sequence characterized by excessive speed of speaking, disorganized sentence structure, and slurred or omitted syllables and sounds. A *language disorder* is a breakdown in the ability to receive, process, or express ideas and information. This disability may exhibit itself in one or more modalities.

Item 12 of Figure 2 is a statement or summary of the student's present level of performance. This includes information on the child's academic achievement, social adaption, prevocational and vocational skills, psychomotor skills, and self-help skills. Educational strengths and weaknesses, compared to his age and grade level, and any other performance strengths and weakness are described in this section.

Item 13 is a statement of the program goals based on the needs of the student. Written descriptions of the goals to be achieved by the end of the school year in regard to the Total Service Plan must be included. The goals should be written in terms of the student and should detail the desired behavior or result.

Item 14 is a list of the specific special education services and/or related services provided by the school and community for the child. The services needed by the child must be determined without regard to the availability of those services. In addition, item 15 is a list of the person(s) responsible for implementing the services described and listed in item 14. For some children, the list may contain only one or two names; however, for other children, the list may include several professionals: special and regular classroom teachers, speech-language pathologist, vision specialist, and so on.

Items 17, 18, and 19 are dates that must be included in the Total Service Plan. Item 17 is the starting date or the date when the student will begin receiving special services. Item 18 is the projected ending date or the estimated date on which the student will complete the program goal. Beginning and ending dates should be entered for each service provided the child. Item 19 is the annual review date or the date that the IEP will be reevaluated. The program goals and the child's progress are reviewed on this date and revisions are made according to the child's needs.

Item 20 (the CST recommendations: methods and materials) allows for suggestions to help implement goals and objectives. This list includes materials and methods, as well as teaching and learning strategies that will help the student reach the proposed program goals. The following are examples of possible recommendations: the amount of time spent in instruction, depending on the child's attention span; the method of presentation and the mode of response the child will use, and any special techniques or games that might facilitate learning.

Item 21 describes the evaluation criteria. The objectives must be evaluated at least once a year. The goals may be evaluated using a formal test instrument or by specific criteria established to effectively measure the child's progress. For example, if the goal was to increase the student's comprehension ability, he or she might be required to answer, in writing, each day, ten questions regarding a story from a specific book.

Item 22 requires the signature of all the CST members. In addition, item 23 provides a space to list the position of each team member. Item 24 requires that each team member check as to whether they agree or disagree with the information set forth in the IEP. Finally, item 25 gives the date of the CST placement meeting. Figure 3 shows a completed Total Service Plan.

The Individual Implementation/Instructional Plan

The second portion of the Individualized Educational Program is known as the Individualized Instructional or Individual Implementation Plan. As its name suggests, the IIP is an additional statement pertaining to the annual goals which have already been identified in the Total Service Plan for the student. Although Public Law 94-142 does not mandate the writing of an IIP in addition to the TSP, many state agencies recommend or require that it be included as a necessary part of the IEP.

In essence, the IIP is a detailed description of the steps and strategies which will be necessary for completion of the goals and

FIGURE 3 Individualized Educational Program: Total Service Plan (Illustrated)

Local Education Agency:
Name and Number __Lexington 5__

School __Oak Knoll Elementary__
Name of Student __Jerry Doe__
Date of Birth __9-5-70__ Age __6-0__ Grade __1__

Description of Educational Placement Recommendations:

	Hrs/Week
Special Education Program Model __Self-contained__	__30__
Regular Education __NA__	__0__

Legal Category of exceptionality (for funding purposes only) __Trainable__
__Mentally Retarded__

Summary of Present Levels of Student Performance:

Jerry has a chronological age of 6-0. His mental age is 3-4 and his language age is 3-0. He has very few self-help skills and his expressive and receptive communication skills are far below his chronological age. IQ testing revealed an approximate score of 45.

Program Goal(s)	Specific Special Education and/or Related Services	Person (s) Responsible For Implementation	Hours Per Week	Starting Date	Projected Ending Date	Annual Review Date (Mo-Yr)	Child Study Team Recommendations: Methods & Materials (if appropriate)	Evaluation Criteria
Jerry will be able to demonstrate the ability to eat, to drink, and to dress independently.	Physical Therapy	Ms. Brown	3	8-21-76	5-21-77	5-77	special cup, use token & verbal reinforcement	Jerry will eat, drink, and dress independently
	Special Ed. Classroom	Ms. Smith	30	8-21-76	5-27-77	5-77		

SOURCE: Adapted by the author from Judy A. Schrag, *Individualized Educational Programming (IEP): A Child Study Team Process.* Hingham, Mass.: Teaching Resources Corp., 1977, p. 25.

FIGURE 3 (*Cont.*) Individualized Educational Program: Total Service Plan (Illustrated)

Child Study Team Members Present

Signature	Position	Agreement with IEP: Total Service Plan (Check appropriate space)		Date of Child Study
		Yes	No	Team Meeting: 5-27-76
Mr. John Hill	Chairman—Study Team	✓		
Mrs. Joanne Smith	Special Educator	✓		
Mrs. G. Wilage	Parent	✓		
Mr. Robert J. Joshua III	Speech/Lang. Pathologist	✓		
Mr. Lucky Brown	Physical Therapist	✓		
Ms. Judy Greene	Media Specialist	✓		

Source: Adapted by the author from Judy A. Schrag, *Individualized Educational Programming (IEP): A Child Study Team Process.* Hingham, Mass.: Teaching Resources Corp., 1977, p. 25.

Program Goals	Specific Education and/or Support Services	Person(s) Responsible	Hours Per Week	Starting Date	Ending Date	Review Date (Mo-Yr)	Child Study Team Recommendations: Methods & Materials	Objective Evaluation Criteria
Student will develop attending skills for auditory and visual stimuli.	Special education classroom	Ms. Smith	30	9-15-76	5-15-77	5-15-77	picture books, "talking books," slides, tapes, records, films	When presented with visual and/or auditory stimuli, the child will be able to attend to the task for at least five minutes
	Speech therapy	Mr. Thomas	5	10- 1-76	5-15-77	5-15-77		
	Library	Ms. Greene	1	10- 1-76	5-15-77	5-15-77		
Student (Jerry) will increase his expressive language skills	Speech/language therapy	Mr. Thomas	4	9-20-76	5-21-77	5-77	Peabody Picture Cards, DLM cards	Given a stimulus, Jerry will respond with the appropriate response.

SOURCE: Adapted by the author from Judy A. Schrag, *Individualized Educational Programming (IEP): A Child Study Team Process.* Hingham, Mass.: Teaching Resources Corp., 1977, p. 25.

objectives identified in the Total Service Plan. For each program or special service listed on the TSP, there will be a specific team member who is responsible for both the development and implementation of an IIP for that area. It is best developed after the initial IEP meetings, and unlike the TSP which is developed from the suggestions of any or all team members, the IIP is constructed by the area specialist who is most qualified to devise a step-by-step approach to the accomplishment of the stated goals.

Several considerations should be made prior to the actual writing of the IIP, the most important of which is careful consideration of the testing and diagnostic procedures which have been obtained. In order to develop specific and measurable objectives, it may be necessary to administer additional formal or informal tests. Public Law 94-142 states that no single test or evaluation procedure may be used to determine the appropriate educational program for a student. One definite benefit of this statement is that each area specialist will have an assortment of tests and test results to refer to before deciding which areas are in greatest need of remediation, and which approaches would be most successful in accomplishing that remediation and ultimately achieving the overall goal which has been set. For example, if the speech-language pathologist was responsible for developing an IIP for the annual goal "to increase expressive language skill," she might choose to include any number of objectives which could eventually lead to an increase in expressive language skills. However, through a careful study of the student's test performances, the speech-language pathologist could identify specific deficit areas which require special attention. These are the areas which should be included in the final IIP.

Another consideration which should be made pertains to goals to be worked on jointly by two or more of the team members. There are many types of program goals which might best be implemented by more than one of the specialists in the IEP team. One such goal would be the development or improvement of attending skills. The responsibility of this goal could be divided between the special education/classroom teacher, the librarian, and the speech-language pathologist. In such a case, each of the three involved team members would be responsible for the development of an IIP.

Although it is likely that each of the specialists will have his or her own idea concerning the accomplishment of the goal, it would be beneficial to the child if there was an attempt to incorporate these ideas into three closely related objectives, or even better, into a single agreed-upon objective or group of objectives which all three specialists can use together to obtain the goal of developing attending skills. Such consistence between specialists will lead to less confusion and ultimately less failure for the child.

After these two areas have been considered, the IIP can be written. As is the case with the Total Service Plan, there is no standard format which must be followed in writing the IIP. It is usually left to the individual agency or school district to develop a workable, usable IIP form. As a result, the forms will vary from district to district; however, each form must include certain necessary components, illustrated in Figure 4.

In completing an IIP, the area specialist should be sure to include the student's full name as it appeared on the TSP, as well as any additional identifying information such as his date of birth, age, grade, and the school he attends (items 2 through 5 of Figure 4). Items 6 through 9 include the signature of the person writing the IIP, the date for initiation of the IEP (usually stated as the date when the form is completed), the established review date, and the responsible local education agency.

Next, it is necessary to restate the program goal as it was stated in the TSP. Some IIP forms require that the goals be numbered to correspond to the order in which they appeared on the Total Service Plan. If, therefore, the goal for which you are responsible appeared third on the Total Service Plan, you will designate the goal as number three on your IIP (item 10 of Figure 4)

Some IIP forms require a statement regarding the student's level of performance. The statement should be clear and understandable so that it may later serve as baseline information in determining the amount of progress the student has made toward obtaining the established objective. Such information can be valuable in deciding whether or not changes are necessary in the strategies or techniques being employed. It is also necessary to include a more specific and detailed description of the stated goal. It must be broken down into objectives or measurable steps (item 11, Figure 4) which, when placed in proper sequence, will enable the child to reach the final

FIGURE 4　Individualized Educational Program: Implementation/Instructional Plan

Name of Student __(1)__　Date of Birth __(2)__　Age __(3)__　Grade __(4)__　School __(5)__

Local Education Agency Name & No. __(6)__

Date of Entry into Program __(7)__　Projected Ending Date __(8)__

__(9)__
(Signature of Implementor Completing this Form)

Program Goal(s)	Implementation/Instructional Objectives	Strategies and/or Techniques	Materials and/or Resources	Date Started	Date Ended	Criteria for Mastery of each Implementation/Instructional Objective
(10)	(11)	(12)	(13)	(14)	(15)	(16)

SOURCE: Adapted by the author from Judy A. Schrag, *Individualized Educational Programming (IEP): A Child Study Team Process.* Hingham, Mass.: Teaching Resources Corp., 1977, p. 25.

more general goal (Figure 5). Included in this statement (use extra forms if necessary) should be a proposed criterion for the mastery of the objective. If, for example, the objective for a student was to name fifty objects when shown those objects or pictures of those objects, the criterion for mastery might be stated as 80 percent accuracy (see Figure 7).

Keep in mind when developing the objectives and establishing the required criteria that they must be realistic. For a child unable to identify *any* objects upon request, it would be an unfortunate mistake to include the identification of fifty objects with 80 percent accuracy as the first objective. The child would most likely be unable to achieve success, and frustration of both the child and the teacher/specialist would be an inevitable result.

Another area required in the completion of an IIP concerns the various strategies and/or techniques (item 12, Figure 4) that will be used to help the student meet the designated objective. An example of strategies used in obtaining skills might include having the student sit in a chair and listen to a five minute story using a headset (Figure 6). Not only will this inform the other specialists of how you are working on a specific area, but it will also enable them to incorporate such strategies into their daily lessons.

Materials and resources to be used in these strategies should also be included in the IIP (item 13, Figure 4). For the above example, this might simply include listing a particular read-along story or group of taped children's stories that will be used. Remember to include strategies and techniques for each objective as well as materials and resources for each strategy.

Finally, to complete the IIP, you will need to identify and record both the date each objective was begun and the date when each was mastered (items 14 and 15, Figure 4).

According to the standard set forth by Public Law 94-142, each handicapped child must have an IEP in effect at the beginning of the school year, and each child should begin receiving services on the first scheduled day of school. For newly identified handicapped children, the IEP meeting is required to be held no later than thirty days after identification. In such cases, the IIP must be written thirty days after the IEP meeting.

The IIP, simply stated, is a portion of the total IEP which is developed by an individual on the IEP team, and which elaborates

FIGURE 5 Individualized Educational Program: Implementation/Instruction/Instructional Plan (Illustrated)

Name of Student ___Jerry Doe___ Date of Birth _9-5-70_ Age _6-0_ Grade _1_ School _Oak K._
Date of Entry into Program ___8-21-76___ Projected Ending Date _5-27-77_

Local Education
Agency
Name & No. _Lexington 5_

(Signature of Implementor Completing this Form)

Program Goal(s)	Implementation/Instructional Objectives	Strategies and/or Techniques	Materials and/or Resources	Date Started	Date Ended	Criteria for Mastery of each Implementation/ Instructional Objective
Jerry will be able to demonstrate the ability to eat, to drink, and to dress by himself.	Jerry will eat with a spoon.	Modeling Verbal commands	Teacher made materials	8-21-76	3-11-77	Each objective will be performed with at least 90% accuracy as judged by the teacher.
	Jerry will drink from a cup.			" "	2- 5-77	
	Jerry will unbutton and button clothes by himself.			" "	4- 9-77	
	Jerry will unzip his pants by himself.			" "	1- 4-77	
	Jerry will put on his mittens by himself.			" "	1- 6-77	
	Jerry will put on and take off his socks by himself.			" "	2- 3-77	
	Jerry will put on his cap by himself			" "	2- 6-77	

SOURCE: Adapted by the author from Judy A. Schrag, *Individualized Educational Programming (IEP): A Child Study Team Process.* Hingham, Mass.: Teaching Resources Corp., 1977, p. 25.

FIGURE 6 Individualized Educational Program: Implementation/Instructional Plan (Illustrated)

Name of Student __Jerry Doe__ Date of Birth __9-5-70__ Age __6-0__ Grade __1__ School __Oak Knoll__

Date of Entry into Program __10-1-76__ Projected Ending Date __5-15-77__

Local Education Agency Name & No. __Lexington 5__

__Jerry Crane Librarian Special__

(Signature of Implementor Completing this Form)

Program Goal(s)	Implementation/Instructional Objectives	Strategies and/or Techniques	Materials and/or Resources	Date Started	Date Ended	Criteria for Mastery of each Implementation/Instructional Objective
Student will develop attending skills for auditory stimuli and visual stimuli.	Student will sit in his seat and listen to a five minute story.	Student will wear headset and sit in a chair while he listens to a five minute story on the tape recorder.	Read-along story	10-1-76	In progress	Student will be able to sit in his seat and listen to a five minute story on at least 9 trials out of 10 (90% accuracy).
	Student will sit in his seat and listen to the teacher read a five minute story to the group.	Student will sit with the group and listen and look at the pictures presented as the teacher reads a story to the group.	Selected story with high interest level	10-8-76	In progress	Student will be able to sit in his seat with a group as the teacher presents a five minute story. He will be able to perform this task with at least 90% accuracy.

SOURCE: Adapted by the author from Judy A. Schrag, *Individualized Educational Programming (IEP): A Child' Study Team Process.* Hingham, Mass.: Teaching Resources Corp., 1977, p. 25.

FIGURE 7 Individualized Educational Program: Implementation/Instructional Plan (Illustrated)

Name of Student __Jerry Doe__   Date of Birth __9-5-70__ Age __6-0__   Grade __1__   School __Oak Knoll__

Local Education Agency Name & No. __Lexington 5__

Date of Entry into Program __9-20-76__   Projected Ending Date __5-21-77__

(Signature of Implementor Completing this Form)

Program Goal(s)	Implementation/Instructional Objectives	Strategies and/or Techniques	Materials and/or Resources	Date Started	Date Ended	Criteria for Mastery of each Implementation/ Instructional Objective
Jerry will increase his expressive language skills.	Jerry will name 50 objects when he is shown that object or a picture of that object.	Jerry will be taught the name of each object individually. The object will be presented and the name given. Verbal cues will be faded gradually.	DLM cards Peabody Picture Cards	9-20-76	In progress	Jerry will name the object or picture of the object with 80% accuracy as judged by the SLP.

SOURCE: Adapted by the author from Judy A. Schrag, *Individualized Educational Programming (IEP): A Child Study Team Process.* Hingham, Mass.: Teaching Resources Corp., 1977, p. 25.

FIGURE 8 Individualized Educational Program: Annual Review

Name of Student __Jerry Doe__ Date of Birth __9-5-70__ Age __6-0__ Grade __1__ School __Oak Knoll Elem.__ Local Education Agency Name & No. __Lexington 5__
Date of Annual Review __5-15-77__

IEP: Total Service Plan and Implementation/Instructional Components:	Level of Appropriateness (Check appropriate space)		Recommended Changes:
	YES	NO	
Special Education Placement	✓		
Regular Education Placement		✓	Library with age group—1 hour weekly
Specific Special Education and/or Related Services	✓		
Program Goal(s)	✓		
Implementation/Instructional Short-term Objective(s)	✓		
Specific Materials and/or Resources	✓		
Specific Teaching Strategies and/or Techniques	✓		
Evaluation Criteria for Completion of Program Goal(s)	✓		
Evaluation Criteria for Completion of Implementation/Instructional Objective(s)	✓		

Child Study Team Members Present		Agreement with Annual Review (Check appropriate space)	
Signature	Position	Yes	No
Mr. John Hill	Chairman—Study Team	✓	
Mrs. Sheila Smith	Special Educator	✓	
Mrs. G. W. Doe Sr.	Parent	✓	
Mr. Heladd J. Horinho III	Speech/Lang. Pathologist	✓	
Mr. Ladajo Brown	Physical Therapist	✓	
Ms. Jenny Greene	Media Specialist	✓	

SOURCE: Adapted by the author from Judy A. Schrag, *Individualized Educational Programming (IEP): A Child Study Team Process.* Hingham, Mass.: Teaching Resources Corp., 1977, p. 25.

on the total program goals. It restates the annual goals, lists instructional objectives to facilitate meeting those goals, and then states the criteria of mastery which are to be met. Although some view this portion of the IEP as being a repetitive and unnecessary amount of additional paper work, others have found that its employment can result in a smooth, more effective means of remediation of the previously identified deficit areas.

IEP Annual Review

A third portion of the IEP process is the IEP Annual Review. To complete this process, the Child Study Team meets again, usually in the late spring, to review the goals set down in the original IEP and determine the child's progress toward the short-term objectives and annual goals. At this point, depending on the child's progress, the CST either revises the original IEP Total Service Plan and the implementation plan, or completes a new Total Service Plan and subsequent IIP. Figure 8 is an example of an IEP Annual Review completed by the CST. Any recommended changes that differ from the original plan must be indicated on the annual review and thus stated on the form.

For some children, at that point in the process the Child Study Team may decide that no further special education services are necessary. The team would then consider whether or not the child should now be placed back into the full-time regular classroom.

In conclusion, the legislature's approach to providing a free, appropriate education for all handicapped children was the passage of Public Law 94-142. At the center of this law is the specification that each handicapped student have on file with the local education agency an Individual. Education Program which consists of three components: the IEP Total Service Plan, the Individual Implementation Plan, and the Annual Review.

Notes

1. Sy Du Bow, "Public Law 94-142," p. 468.
2. Ibid.
3. Stan Dublinske, "PL 94-142," p. 335.
4. Ibid., p. 336.

116   Ellen C. Fagan

References

Barbacovi, Don R., and Clelland, Richard W. *Public Law 94-142*. Arlington, Va.: American Association of School Administrators, 1978.
Bierly, K. "Answers to the Questions You're Asking." *Instructor* 87 (April 1978): 62.
Calhoun, Mary Lunne, et al. *Implementing IEPs in Regular and Resource Classrooms*. Unpublished MS, Winthrop College, University of South Carolina, 1979.
Downey, Morgan. "Conduct for the Due Process Hearing." *ASHA* 22 (May 5, 1980): 332-34.
Dublinske, Rosemary, and Healy, William C. "PL 94-142: Questions and Answers for the Speech/Language Pathologist and Audiologist." *ASHA* 20 (March 1978): 188-205.
Dublinske, Stan. "Pl 94-142: Due Process Decisions." *ASHA* 22 (May 5, 1980): 335-38.
Du Bow, Sy. "Public Law 94-142." *American Annals of the Deaf* 122 (October 1977): 468-69.
Fagan, Ellen C. "The Librarian's Role: Developing and Implementing an Individual Educational Program (IEP) for the Handicapped Child." Paper presented at School Library Media Services to the Handicapped Workshop, University of Mississippi, Oxford, Miss.: August 1979.
Kaye, Nancy L., and Aserlind, Ray. "The IEP: the Ultimate Process." *Journal of Special Education* 13 (Summer 1979): 137-43.
Klein, Nancy K. "Least Restrictive Alternative: An Educational Analysis." *Education and Training of the Mentally Retarded* 13 (February 1978): 102-14.
Motz, Patricia A. "The School-Aged Child, the Law, and the School Nurse." *Journal of School Health* 48 (November 1978): 568.
Palfrey, Judith S., et al. "New Directions in the Evaluation and Education of Handicapped Children." *New England Journal of Medicine* 298 (April 13, 1978): 819-24.
Parks, A. Lee, and Rousseau, Marilyn K. *The Public Law Supporting Mainstreaming: A Guide for Teachers and Parents*. Austin, Tex.: Learning Concepts, 1977.
Schrag, Judy A. *IEP Media Kit*. Austin, Tex.: Learning Concepts, 1977.
Torres, Scottie. *Special Education Administrative Policies Manual*. Reston, Va.: Council for Exceptional Children, 1977.
Turnbull, Ann P.; Strickland, B. B.; and Brantley, J. C. *Developing and Implementing IEPs*. Columbus, Ohio: Charles E. Merrill Publishing Co., 1978.

6

FUNDING MEDIA SERVICES FOR HANDICAPPED CHILDREN

Kieth C. Wright

Many of the programs and materials suggested elsewhere in this book are expensive. Often the question will arise, "How can we possibly try that idea?" Funds are available from various public and private organizations. Sources of information for grants and programs and some criteria for developing and evaluating grant or project requests follow.

Principles of Funding Programs and Services

NO SPECIAL SERVICES. The purpose of seeking additional funds is to offer handicapped children as near to regular services as possible. This concept is clearly implied by the "least restrictive environment" language of Public Law 94-142 and by many parts of the 504 regulations forbidding discrimination in educational services offered to handicapped children.

The goal of the school media program is to provide access to the right information in the appropriate format for each child. Because of a variety of physical and/or mental-emotional difficulties, the traditional formats of print and audiovisual materials may need modification. In some situations the network of already existing services can be utilized to obtain appropriate free materials, such as

talking books from the National Library Service for the Blind and
Physically Handicapped, or Capital Films for the Deaf from the
Capital Films for the Deaf Distribution Center, 5034 Wisconsin
Avenue, Washington, D.C. 20016.

It may be necessary to modify materials in terms of format
(caption slides for a slide-tape series so that the deaf child can use
the set), or to acquire special equipment such as additional cassette
recorders for visually impaired children to use for note-taking, or a
closed circuit television system or other enlarging device for
reading print materials or studying maps and charts. In these cases,
additional funds may be needed. The funding request should
emphasize that the sources already available have been used and
additional funds are needed to provide regular and appropriate
media services to all the children.

DOUBLE AND TRIPLE DUTY. Historically, materials in special
formats, special equipment, and special techniques have been
developed with a specific disability situation in mind. Often federal
legislation written for a specific handicapped group excluded other
groups from using those services or products. For example, talking
books were available to the adult blind for a number of years. Only
after some time did people realize that such materials were also
useful to visually impaired children as well as people who could not
use regular print format because of physical disabilities other than
blindness. Captioned films made for deaf people can also be used
for bilingual education and a variety of learning disabilities.
Various nonverbal communication techniques have been used with
groups other than the original intended audience. Communication
devices are now used in a variety of physical and emotional disability settings, and sign language systems originally used only
with the deaf are being used with mentally handicapped and emotionally disturbed children.

The principle to remember is the economy of double or triple
use. Many materials selected for one disability situation can be
used for others. High interest/low vocabulary materials are not just
for EMR students; they may also be used in a variety of learning
disability settings. Large print books or magnification may make
materials accessible to wheelchair-bound children because the

materials can be clearly seen at a distance. The use of materials should never be limited to only one intended audience. Be innovative and experimental.

LOOK BEYOND YOUR OWN CIRCLE. Most good media center specialists have developed expertise at ferreting out appropriate materials from a wide variety of sources. Building on a base preservice selection and library school courses, media specialists continue to develop sources to meet the specific educational needs of the children and teachers in their school. They are now faced with a new situation with a far wider set of educational needs, particularly in the areas of materials format and specific information content.

Media specialists need to develop contact with other professional persons who have had experience with handicapped children. The resource room specialists found in some schools can provide a wealth of special education techniques, diagnostic abilities, and specifically formatted materials. School psychologists, rehabilitation center staff members, visiting school-system specialists, and local health service personnel are some people who may have helpful information to share. In the past, many services to handicapped children were considered "special" services, and the professionals who provided them were isolated from the mainstream of our education system. The new requirement placed on local education agencies demands that media specialists and teachers build bridges with other professionals in the community. Often these professionals will know of sources of material and equipment that can assist the media specialist in selection to meet specific needs. B. J. Eckstein gives a list of state agency directors of mental health programs, vocational rehabilitation, and special education, as well as regional and local federal offices of the Department of Health and Human Services, the Community Services Administration, and Federal Information Centers. If media specialists do not have local community contacts, these offices at the state level or the federal regional offices may be able to refer them. Velleman also gives a number of contact points in her book.

DON'T BE A CHAMELEON. Foundations have goals for their grant programs. Federal legislation which authorizes grants, and the regulations later developed by agencies for evaluating applications, are usually very specific about the target audience, types of acceptable activity, and eligible agency. Do not be tempted to modify your basic program goals and objectives or stretch your own competencies just to get funds. The greatest success for funding usually comes from foundations and funding agencies whose goals, programs, and audiences are similar to your own. Changing your program, dreaming up new projects, or having to develop needed skills can detract from your basic purpose of providing appropriate information in appropriate formats. This does not mean that one should "keep on keeping on" in the same old ways with the same old programs and materials. If additional funds can strengthen your basic goals and objectives while helping to develop new strategies, materials, and services, fine.

Sources of Information on Grants and Programs

Some basic guidance on how to develop funding proposals and seek funds may be helpful. F. S. Buchtel's "Blueprint for Getting a Grant for Research" is written by the former director of research services of Western Michigan University. J. Dermer's *How to Raise Funds from Foundations* is a general "how to" for all types of agencies and services. His *How to Write Successful Foundation Presentations* is by the same publisher. Fuller and Associates and the Regional Young Adult Project's *Bread Game* is published by the Glide Foundation group—past masters at specific fund raising techniques for social service and educational projects. Here they share their savvy. This book may be out of print, look for it! J. S. Green's *Grantsmanship* is a very practical step-by-step approach with illustrations from both foundation publications and government documents. It is published by the same group that publishes the *Annual Register of Grant Support*. Beyond background information, media specialists need to have some basic reference tools. Publication information for these and other works discussed in this chapter can be found in the reference section. This list is by no means exhaustive, and new tools and sources will become available as the process of seeking funding becomes more competitive.

Sources of Information on Foundation Funding

The *Annual Register of Grant Support* lists multiple types of grant support, from awards through conference grants. Arrangement is by broad subject categories with organizational, personal, and geographic indexes. The register includes information on foundations and government funding sources, as well as other business and professional sources. The listing for each entry includes a brief description of the agency (name, address, telephone number, date of funding, formal title of program). Specific programs include the type and purpose of each grant, who is eligible, funds provided for each award, total number of applicants in the last year, number of awards, and total dollar amount of support for the most recent year. Application information includes deadlines, major personnel of the agency, where to address inquiries, any legal basis of the program, and special information.

The *Bowker Annual of Library and Booktrade Information* includes lists of grants compiled from *Foundation News* (see below) arranged in two sections: an alphabetical list of foundations, and a subject list of grantees giving names, and amount and purpose of grants. Different annual editions also discuss major government and corporate grants—check the index under "grants, library." Often special topic chapters also include funding source and project description information.

The *Foundation Directory*, a publication of the Foundation Center, gives a very brief description of nonprofit, nongovernmental organizations in the United States having assets of $500,000 or more, or which made grants of more than $25,000 in one year. The directory is alphabetically arranged by foundation name and gives the name, address, date of funding, purpose, activities, financial data, contact person (initials), number of grants given, and average amount of grants for each foundation listed. A subject index gives page numbers only. The Foundation Center collects information on foundations, and publishes a number of information pieces, including the *Foundation Center Source Book Profiles*, *Foundation Grants Index*, and *Foundation News*.

The *Foundation Center Source Book Profiles*, bimonthly since 1978/79, updates the *Foundation Directory* with information on new foundations, revised entries for those already listed, brief abstracts from foundation annual reports, bibliographies, an acquisition list of the center's library, and announcements concerning center information services. *Foundation Grants Index* is an accumulative listing of foundation grants which is updated by *Foundation News* in a section called *Foundation Grants Index*. *Foundation News*, edited by P. W. Kennedy, is a bimonthly newsletter on foundations, their activities and philosophy. It also includes news about book reviews and a calendar of deadlines and activities.

In addition to publications, the Foundation Center libraries maintain a computer data bank of foundation grants which can be searched by name, amount, and key word. There is a charge for custom searches, but on-site assistance from the national libraries (including computer searches) is available free of charge. Income tax information from foundations filing form 1099 is available on microfiche.

There are cooperating collections in fifty states, Mexico, and Puerto Rico, a list of which can be found in Appendix IV. Almost every media specialist will have relatively easy access to a cooperating library and should not consider applying to any foundation without researching the foundation's purposes and past activities.

Sources of Information on Government Funding

Catalog of Federal Domestic Assistance lists over a thousand domestic assistance programs and activities which are administered by some sixty-five federal agencies and departments. The listing is indexed by interest areas in broad categories and each entry explains who is eligible to apply, application procedures, what reports will be required, financial data of authorization and appropriation by Congress, regional information contacts, and so on. Other related programs are listed at the end of each entry.

The *Commerce Business Daily* is a daily list of U.S. government procurement invitations, contract awards, and sales of property. Many of these are Requests For Proposals (RFPs) or Requests For Services (RFSs). Most entries will be of limited use to media specialists except where requested literature searches, other information services, and library contract services may indicate new and emerging interests of specific federal agencies or regional offices. *Federal Notes* is a newsletter covering federal programs and grants with an emphasis on requests for special service proposals.

The *Federal Register* is a U.S. government publication listing all proposed administrative and policy changes of federal agencies including rules, definitions, and deadlines for all grant programs. Often the earliest information available on annual deadline dates and new, or revised, application procedures or eligibility criteria will be found in the *Federal Register*.

Developing and Evaluating a Grant or Project Proposal

While not intended as a full course in proposal writing and evaluation, some criteria which will be useful to anyone beginning the process for the first time are presented below.

Foundation Proposals

After discovering the purposes and previous grant activities of a foundation, media specialists need to ask themselves: Do we have projects, ideas, and needs related to the interest areas of the foundation? What have other funded projects done? Often a project summary or report can be obtained. What is unique about the project proposal in terms of new research areas, population served, needs of those people, or characteristics of the school and community? Who can cosponsor this idea?

Once such questions are answered, the media specialist will need to write a draft of the proposal. The draft should be developed and evaluated in light of the following criteria: (1) The proposal contains a clear, concise statement of what the project will accomplish. In education it is easy to use language currently popular in educational circles that means nothing to outsiders. Avoid high level abstractions, vague generalities, and pious platitudes. Remember that most foundations have boards made up of intelligent business people who will want to know what they are getting for the money they invest.

(2) The project proposal will contain evidence of how the project will be evaluated by the project staff, by their clients, and by some qualified outside evaluator. Evaluation should be built into the design of the project, not tacked on at the end.

(3) The need for the project will be clearly and specifically stated in the proposal and supported by information, dates, and letters from other professionals in the school and community. Do not allow your "ownership" of a project idea to keep you from discussing it with others, making modifications, and gaining support.

(4) Unique skills, experiences, or capabilities of the institution, the media center, or the staff will be clearly stated. If your school, your center, or you have uniquely suited talents to do the job, say so.

(5) The project proposal budget will be clearly presented and all parts justified. Be sure that the money requested is really needed; that every penny can be justified; and that there is a means of accounting for how the money is spent. If the school, Local Education Agency (LEA), or State Education Agency (SEA) are also supporting the project, or if there is other outside funding, be sure to mention it in the budget section so that the foundation can see that others value the project enough to help fund it.

(6) The time period for project proposal will be finite. Never make a vague, continuing proposal. If the project goes beyond one year, be sure that an outline is included showing how each year's project will benefit from the previous year's experience. Where possible, decreased funding in later years of the proposal should be considered in order to demonstrate the school's own investment in the project—picking up more and more of the costs. Be sure the proposal mentions in some detail what will happen once the project funding stops. Who will pick up the costs? How will the findings be disseminated? What other sources of later support seem possible?

The media specialist now has a draft of a proposal idea written. This draft does not need to be long or fully detailed, but the basic outline is essential prior to the next step. Once the ideas are firmly on paper, the media specialist can proceed to arouse foundation interest. Often a personal visit to local or regional foundations can be arranged by writing a simple letter requesting an appointment and including a brief abstract of the proposal. Obviously the media specialist cannot travel nationally to seek funds, but often the *Foundation Directory* will indicate the contact person for prospective grants. Where the media specialist cannot visit personally, a letter of inquiry should explain why this foundation is likely to be interested in the proposal, and include a brief description of the project (one- or two-page outline style), with the name, address, and telephone number of the media center contact person. Be sure this letter is brief, businesslike, and that anything said can be substantiated. *Foundation Directory* or other sources may list times of the year or deadlines for grants—always observe these.

If the media specialist writes to fifteen foundations, at least one or two will probably request more information, or possibly offer to fund the proposal. Negative responses are much more common than positive responses, and even positive responses will be guarded. Usually there will be a specific format for proposals; often a meeting will be suggested. Follow up on even very cautious letters or telephone calls. Check the list of officers or trustees of local area foundations for a familiar name, in order to discuss the proposal with that person and see if they can become your advocate with the foundation. If the letter says, "we are interested, but have no funds now," the media specialist will want to write a brief thank-you note, and follow up at a later date. "Last year we submitted a proposal on _____, and would like to give you an update on our project."

Once the media specialist gets to the final proposal stage, steps should be taken to make sure the following information is given: what the project will do, and what it hopes to accomplish in what time frame; who will be responsible and involved (include vitae); how the project will be evaluated; how funds will be spent and accounted for; how results will be disseminated (to reflect favor on the school and the foundation); and what future plans are now in place to meet the identified needs after the foundation funds end.

Government Proposals

Many of the criteria listed for foundation proposals will also apply to government proposals; however, there are some unique problems with government proposals.

PROCEDURES AND DEADLINES. The federal or state government has thousands of applicants, and the process of determining eligibility—who meets the criteria or regulations established by Congress—and how the proposals will be evaluated is lengthy. This process is complicated by the fact that deadlines seem always to be imminent. Thus, the applicant must quickly determine the focus of the announcement, how proposals will be rated, whether or not the school or media center is eligible to apply, and how many state and regional federal office endorsements will be required. Meeting the deadline can mean writing six to eight months in advance for information on your proposal.

COMPLEX FORMS, BUDGETS, AND ASSURANCES. Congress and the executive branch have increasingly used their funding capability to assure compliance with federal laws in the areas of civil rights, environment, and so on. Sections 503 and 504 of the Rehabilitation Act of 1973 are good examples of such efforts. All federal proposals must give assurance of meeting the requirements of these laws and regulations. The same assurances are needed concerning compliance with the Civil Rights Act, Title IX (equity for women). Anyone facing the folder of forms and attached explanations for the first time may decide not to proceed. Even more discouraging are the budget forms which require the same information on three to five different forms, often with totals by type, by project year, and by categories. *Do not give up.* Read the entire federal packet through. Some sections of every Federal proposal are the same, and often these sections can be developed once and then kept on file for later applications. The school principal or superintendent will be required to sign a number of forms. Someone else in the school system probably applies for federal dollars for some purpose. See if they can translate the sections that are technical in nature.

With government proposals, media specialists will need to add several new criteria to those already mentioned under foundation proposals: (1) The project proposal will identify the problem or situation as important to more than a local or regional area. The federal government is concerned by law with the entire population in all sections of the country. Proposals should be relevant to other settings and perhaps to other populations. The more national impact a proposal has, the better the chances of funding.

(2) The proposal will show evidence of knowledge of what has been done in the area and what is now being done. Do not suggest an idea or project that has been tried over and over. Do a good literature search through the *Educational Resources Information Centers* (ERIC) system. If the media specialist has access to on-line reference services, a search can be done on the topic to see who else has been or is working in the same general area. If the media specialist can afford it, computer searching should not be limited to ERIC, but should also include *Psychological Abstracts, National Technical Information Services* (NTIS), *Dissertation Abstracts,* and other appropriate data base. Some local and state education agencies provide such on-line search services. Manual searches in a good research reference library can also yield good results.

(3) The project proposal will give evidence of knowledge of the size, complexity, and nature of the problem addressed. If the media specialist can quantify anything, it should be done. For instance, how many persons need the service and don't have it (locally, statewide, nationally)? What other agencies are meeting part of the need? Have these agencies documented an unmet need? Why do you think your proposal will change all of these facts?

(4) The project proposal will clearly define who will do what and who is responsible. Carefully spell out the way the project will be managed and give full vitae of everyone involved. Be sure that one individual is designated project director and responsible for budget, reports, and staff.

(5) The project proposal will be designed to allow for client evaluation and project modification, internal evaluation, and external evaluation. It is important that evaluation procedures be carefully explained and that measurable empirical procedures be used whenever possible. For example, if the project involves staff training of teachers and aids, the media specialist should be sure to have an evaluation instrument for each session and for the series as a whole, as well as some means of using individual session evaluation to improve later sessions. Every evaluation process should include the *target group* of clients. If the media specialist is offering a service to handicapped students and their families, were the students and families involved in the design of the service and will the project process allow for their feedback throughout? Every proposal is strengthened if the budget includes funds for an external

professional evaluator known in the field, whose evaluation will carry some weight.

(6) The proposal will give details on the *cost sharing* activities of the institution which is making the application. What is the home institution contributing? Be specific about commitments of time, space, equipment, facilities, advice, and money. If the SEA is contributing consultation or evaluation time or leadership for staff development, include that information.

(7) The proposal will include plans for project continuation and further dissemination of results. A project proposal which has built-in processes for dissemination of results, materials developed, or ideas for further research is a better proposal. Never let a government agency think its money will be used without visible results. Always have a plan for continuing on some modified basis with home-institution support.

These suggestions have been included to assist media specialists in the process of evaluating their draft proposals. It is important to remember that the only real test of a proposal to a foundation or the government is to submit it. Even if the proposal fails, the media specialist can learn a great deal and should follow up with the foundation or agency to find out *why* the proposal was not funded. The government must provide a copy of the evaluator's comments if requested. If possible, the media specialist should meet with the staff of the foundation or agency to discuss the reasons why the project was rejected and to seek ways of improving future proposals. Learn from your mistakes, and good luck!

References

Annual Register of Grant Support. Chicago: Marquis Academic Media, 1977, 1978.

Bowker Annual of Library and Booktrade Information. New York: Bowker, annual.

Brodsky, J., ed. *Swipe File.* 2nd. ed. Washington, D.C.: Taft Products, Inc., 1976.

Buchtel, F. S. "Blueprint for Getting a Grant for Research." *College Management* 6 (March 1971): 2021.

California Advisory Council on Vocational Education. *Barrier and Bridge: An Overview of Vocational Services Available for Handicapped Citizens.* Sacramento: Dept. of General Services, Publication Section, n.d.

Catalog of Federal Domestic Assistance. Washington, D.C.: Office of Management and Budget, Superintendent of Documents, annual.

Commerce Business Daily. Washington, D.C.: Department of Commerce, daily.

Dermer, J. *How to Raise Funds from Foundations.* New York: Public Service Materials Center, 1972.

Eckstein, B. J. *Handicapped Funding Directory*, 2d ed. Oceanside, N.Y.: Research Grant Guide, 1979-1980.

Federal Notes, ed. Wallace Breitman. Saratoga, Calif., biweekly.

Federal Register. Washington, D.C.: Superintendent of Documents, daily.

Federal Research Report, ed. L. Eserer. Silver Spring, M.D.: Business Publishers, Inc., weekly.

Foundation Directory, 7th ed., ed. M. O. Lewis. New York: Foundation Center. Distributed by Columbia University Press, New York, 1979.

Foundation News, ed. P. W. Kennedy. New York: Foundation Center, bimonthly.

Fuller and Associates, and Regional Young Adult Project. *The Bread Game.* San Francisco: Glide Publications, n.d.

Green, J. S. *Grantsmanship: Money and How to Get It.* Orange, N.J.: Academic Media, 1973.

Krathwohl, D. R. *How to Prepare a Research Proposal.* Syracuse: Syracuse University Bookstore, 1966.

Mayer, R. A. "Grantsmanship." *Library Journal* 97 (July 1972): 2348-50.

Vanderheiden, G. C. *Non-Vocal Communication Resource Book.* Baltimore: University Park Press, 1978.

Velleman, Ruth A. *Serving Physically Disabled People: An Information Handbook for All Libraries.* New York: Bowker, 1979.

Zallen, H., and Zallen, E. M. *Ideas Plus Dollars: Research Methodology and Funding.* Norman, Okla.: Academic World, 1976.

7

NATIONAL LIBRARY SERVICES FOR THE BLIND AND PHYSICALLY HANDICAPPED

JoEllen Ostendorf

Most people are vaguely aware of the term "talking books," and picture an elderly person with cataracts bent over a phonograph listening to the Bible. Unfortunately, only one-third of the people in the United States who are eligible for talking book library service are aware of its availability and make use of the materials and equipment. Children and young adults are the group most seriously affected by this lack of awareness since recorded books are what may enable visually impaired students to keep pace with their classmates. A large quantity of materials is available to handicapped children, but it is the responsibility of teachers and librarians to inform parents and students of the services to which they are entitled.

Best known of the services available to the handicapped is the talking book library program of the Library of Congress in connection with many libraries across the United States. This program has been the basis of many other programs for the handicapped which often utilize the equipment distributed through the Library of Congress by developing compatible materials on cassettes and discs. As the foremost library in the world for the blind and physically handicapped, the Library of Congress has initiated many innovative concepts and subsidized many research projects to

develop alternative forms of reading. "Library" is perhaps a mis-
nomer since the services offered through libraries across the
country in cooperation with the Library of Congress program go
far beyond those referred to in conjunction with a conventional
public or school library. Talking book libraries exist to serve a
broader scope and plane of users than that of traditional types of
libraries.

Library services to the handicapped are relatively recent when
compared to the number of years libraries have been in existence.
Lack of a standard form of nonwritten communication for the blind
and others who cannot use conventional print was a major obsta-
cle. Even after Louis Braille devised his system of forty-three raised
dots in 1829, the ensuing argument over which variation should be
adopted in the English-speaking world continued until 1932. Only a
few libraries had begun establishing braille reading rooms by the
turn of the century. In 1897, John Russell Young, the librarian of
Congress, conceived the idea of a national library program.
Thanks to his farsightedness, the groundwork was laid for what is
today known as the National Library Service for the Blind and
Physically Handicapped (NLS). Not until the 1930s, however, was
the Library of Congress given the federal legislation to expand the
program. On March 3, 1931, the Pratt-Smoot Bill became law,
providing the Library of Congress with $100,000 to make braille
books available to blind adults and authorizing the establishment
of eighteen regional centers or libraries for the distribution of these
materials. This new service of the Library of Congress was called
the Division for the Blind and Physically Handicapped until 1978
when the rapidly growing services and budget of the division
caused the name to be changed to the National Library Service for
the Blind and Physically Handicapped. It was now truly a library
capable of serving all eligible United States residents.

During the 1930s technology reached the point where the phonograph became a common part of many households, familiarizing
people with musical recordings being produced on discs. In 1934
the idea of adapting these discs for book narration was developed
and the original talking book was born. From the beginning of the
Library of Congress talking book program, free machines were
loaned to eligible readers. The first of the talking book machines

weighed twice as much as present models and required constant maintenance. Needles had to be replaced after playing each record and the motor needed to be oiled every four months. They became so popular that soon more people were using talking books than braille books, a trend which still continues today.

When the program was originally conceived under the Pratt-Smoot Bill, it provided only for the blind adult, but in 1952 the word "adult" was dropped, thus enabling children to benefit from the talking book program. Physically handicapped persons were included in the program in 1966, and in 1974 persons with reading disabilities resulting from organic dysfunction were added. The talking book library service as it exists today at national, state, and local levels is quite recent.

Talking Book Library Service

What are talking books? Talking books are conventional print books which have been narrated on open-reel tape and then con-verted into either a disc or cassette. Recorded books contain the verbatim text of printed books—if there is strong language and explicit descriptions of sex in the printed book, there is strong language and explicit descriptions of sex in the recorded version. No attempt is made to edit the text as is done in some commercially available recordings. Copyright permission must be obtained from the publisher or author before the material can be recorded. At the national level, narrators or readers are often professional actors and actresses, while materials done at the state or local level are usually narrated by volunteers who have been carefully screened to keep the quality of the recordings as high as possible. All materials are monitored for errors by a person who sits outside the sound-proof recording booth and follows the text of the book while the narrator reads. Often the recording is checked again for errors by a reviewer who listens to the finished product and compares it with the text. Emphasis is on quality and accuracy. Listening to a book is quite different from reading a book. A great deal of respons-ibility is placed on the narrator to present the book in a true and interesting manner without overacting or distorting the text of the author. Most narrators use a different tone of voice for each of the main characters to help the listener identify who is speaking, particularly when there is an exchange of conversation which a sighted person would identify in the printed text.

Talking books produced by NLS are distributed in regional and subregional libraries across the country, who in turn, mail them to users. Originally there were only eighteen libraries established in 1931 under the Pratt-Smoot Bill; today there are over 160 regional and subregional libraries. All states except North Dakota are served by a regional library. Several states with large populations, such as California, Michigan, and Ohio, have two regional libraries. Guam, the Virgin Islands, and Puerto Rico also receive talking books through the Library of Congress program. United States citizens living abroad are served through the Overseas Section within NLS. Machines with special voltages are available and a cassette machine using solar power was recently developed for an American living in the Amazon!

Many states have established subregional libraries within their service areas for larger population sites to provide more local, personal service. For example, the regional library in Georgia is located in Atlanta; Georgia has thirteen subregional libraries including ones in Athens, Augusta, and Savannah. Subregional libraries report to the regional library in the states. Besides being a part of the NLS network, regional libraries are often a part of state library commissions or state commissions for the blind. NLS supplies the books, machines, brochures, and catalogs, while state agencies provide the facilities and operating expenses of the departments.

As an alternative to subregional libraries, some states work through their public libraries. Such is the case in Mississippi, where the Library Commission has negotiated sublending agency agreements with the public libraries allowing them to maintain a supply of talking book machines and a deposit collection of talking books. Thus these libraries always have the materials to provide talking book library service to people in their communities.

Until 1974, talking books and talking book machines were distributed directly from NLS to regional libraries, but a readership growth of over 400 percent from 1966 to 1974 and the addition of more regional and subregional libraries no longer made this practical. For this reason multistate centers were established to serve a geographic area of approximately thirteen states. Their major function is to serve as deposits for NLS materials and to provide backup services. Multistate centers house extra catalogs and brochures, extra copies of books in the NLS collection, and maintain small collections of materials produced in limited quantities. Four multistate centers were established by 1977 serving the North, South, Midwest, and West.

Library services to the blind and other physically handicapped persons through the NLS program are performed by working together to supplement and complement the services offered by others. Library service to the handicapped must be a shared responsibility. Public libraries have too long had the attitude that they exist only to serve the sighted, while school libraries have found they are inadequately prepared to serve the influx of handicapped students that are being mainstreamed into their schools. Libraries must realize that they exist to meet the needs of all persons, not only the able-bodied majority. Numerous services do exist for the handicapped and teachers, librarians, and parents must take advantage of them.

Applications for talking book library service are available through regional, subregional, and public libraries. Information requested on the application includes name, address, telephone, date of birth, sex, type of handicap, type of equipment needed (that is, phonograph and/or cassette machine), and reading preferences. Those who are eligible include: (1) blind and legally blind persons whose visual acuity with correcting lenses is 20/200 or less or whose widest diameter of visual field subtends an angular distance of no greater than twenty degrees; (2) visually impaired persons who are certified as unable to read standard printed material; (3) physically handicapped persons who are unable to use standard print due to physical limitations; and (4) persons having a reading disability resulting from organic dysfunction and of sufficient severity to prevent their reading printed materials in a normal manner. In short, anyone who cannot read or hold a book in a conventional manner is eligible for talking book library service. This includes persons with arthritis, rheumatism, stroke victims, persons with dyslexia, or those born with birth defects, such as no arms. Persons with cerebral palsy or muscular dystrophy are also eligible. It must be emphasized, however, that not all physically handicapped persons are eligible for this service. Paraplegics, for example, would not be eligible since their handicap is not such that it would prevent them from reading or holding a book in a conventional manner. Illiterates are not eligible for the program since the use of talking books would, in effect, promote their illiteracy by making it unnecessary for them to learn to read. Illiteracy programs have been established in most states to serve this group. Mentally retarded persons are not eligible for the program, although often an accompanying physical disability does qualify them.

Confidentiality is strictly maintained; names of those using the talking book library service are never given out. Some parents, even with assurance from regional librarians, refuse to register their children for talking books for fear their names would appear on some list of handicapped children. Parents of dyslexic children seem to be particularly sensitive to this. It must be emphasized that libraries are prevented by federal law through their contract with NLS to give out names of users.

All applications must be certified by a "competent authority," which in the case of blindness, visual impairment, or other physical handicap, is defined to include the following: doctors of medicine, doctors of osteopathy, optometrists, ophthalmologists, registered nurses, therapists, and the professional staff of hospitals, institutions, and public or welfare agencies. This includes social workers, caseworkers, counselors, rehabilitation teachers, and superintendents. Professional librarians may certify applications as well. Reading disabilities, such as dyslexia, can only be certified by a medical doctor.

Applictions for talking book library service are of two types, individual and institutional. Individual application means the user is issued talking books and machines and is responsible for using the machines and materials in a proper manner. Institutional service enables nursing homes, hospitals, and schools to take advantage of the talking book program and expand the activities and programs they offer to their patients or students. All institutional applications must be certified by the director of the agency applying for library service. Applicants within an institution who will be using the service must be listed on the application, and those with reading disabilities must have a doctor's statement attached.

Institutions are issued several machines and deposit collections of talking books, with the suggestion that they rotate them on a quarterly basis to make new titles available to readers. Institutional service can be effectively adapted to the needs of the organization. In some cases, users could conceivably be served as individuals and also through an institution. For example, children in a special education class are eligible for talking book library service. The teacher registers the class as an institution and receives talking book services. The children can also be signed up on individual applications using their home addresses so they have material at both home and school. Cooperation between parents and teachers is highly desirable. Sometimes parents do not want to bother with helping the child, so the teacher may assume responsibility for ordering and returning the talking books. Various ways exist in which talking book service can be established. Regardless of whether the user is signed up as an individual or through an institution, the primary concern must be meeting the person's needs with the greatest convenience and ease. If assistance or supervision is a continual requirement, this must also be taken into account. It is highly recommended that institutions assign one person to supervise the materials and assist with their use, thus enabling that person to become familiar with the materials available and the needs of the people in the institution using the service.

A common misconception concerning talking books is that the only books recorded are the Bible and literary classics. This certainly is not true. Patrons of the talking book library service are just as likely to read a bestseller as is someone who uses the public library. Recorded books include popular fiction and nonfiction titles as well as other materials found in any public library. Recorded books appear several months after the print edition is published. From any list of fiction bestsellers one will find that approximately 85 percent have been or are in the process of being recorded, and for those on a nonfiction list the rate is about 65 percent. Some nonfiction books which are heavily illustrated are not appropriate for the recording program, but all which are found suitable are recorded as soon as possible.

Books considered for recording are reviewed by the Collection and Development Section of NLS and an attempt is made to record all appropriate bestsellers. Other books are chosen on the basis of needs expressed by consumers and network libraries. A committee made up of users and librarians meets yearly on regional and national levels to discuss what types of materials are needed so that the NLS may best serve the majority of the users. Major recommendations of the 1979-1980 committee included more travel and guide books, popular authors, handicrafts, school subjects, and world literature. Recommendations for juvenile materials included more action stories, biographies, and science books. Suggestions for young adults included more fantasy, science fiction, and classics.

The NLS collection contains many types of materials including mysteries, westerns, historical novels, romances, and so on. Many children's books are produced each year ranging from ABC books to classics such as "Peter Rabbit" and the Nancy Drew, Hardy Boys, and Tom Swift books. Adventure and space stories are popular juvenile items and include *Johnny Tremaine* and *Star Wars*. Newbery and Caldecott Award winners are recorded each year so handicapped children can "read" them along with their contemporaries. NLS has recently begun producing a limited number of recordings in foreign languages such as Spanish, French, Italian, and German. Juvenile books are also included in the foreign language productions.

In addition to books, a number of magazines are also recorded. Adult magazines include *Reader's Digest, National Geographic, Good Housekeeping, Sports Illustrated,* and *Ebony.* Some children's and young adults' magazines are *Boy's Life, Jack and Jill, Ranger Rick,* and *Seventeen.* In 1980, the Children's Magazine Program consisted of *National Geographic World, Ranger Rick,* and *Jack and Jill* in disc format. At the end of each year subscribers vote for their favorite magazines; the two receiving the greatest number of votes are offered on a continuing basis. Those who sign up for the Young Adult Magazine Program receive a different magazine each month in cassette format. The 1980 program included *Hit Parader*, *Hot Rod*, *Scholastic Scope*, *Seventeen*, *Teen*, and *Young Athlete*. Institutions, particularly schools, can also sign up to receive these materials.

Music services are available in addition to recorded books. NLS's music section is only for the serious musician and does not supply musical recordings such as Lawrence Welk or other popular types. The Music Services Unit was established in 1962 and has become the major source of scores, textbooks, and other instructional materials in various formats. Materials are loaned directly from the Music Services Unit of NLS and are not distributed through regional libraries as are talking books. Basically educational in nature, the collection includes scores, librettos, hymnals, music history, and instructional materials on how to play various instruments. Materials are compatible to the machines utilized for the talking books and are available in braille, disc, cassette, large print, or a special combination of braille, cassette, and large print. Volunteers are available to produce braille, recorded, or large print music transcription for specially requested material which has not already been produced. A specially trained reference staff is available to answer questions on all aspects of music. Periodicals produced by the music section and available to eligible readers include *Music Journal*, *Stereo Review*, and *Musical Mainstream*. There is no age limit on the use of this material.

Upon receipt of a properly certified application at the talking book library, books and equipment are issued. All talking books are mailed with a reversible mailing label; the user's name is on one side, the library's name on the other. To return the book, the user turns the label over and mails the book. In 1904, an act of Congress was passed which permitted free mailing of talking book materials. Postal workers are required by this law to deliver materials to a user's address, but are not required to pick the materials up at the user's home, although many do so of their own accord. Large print materials may also be mailed, "Free Matter for the Blind and Physically Handicapped."

All readers receive a subscription to *Talking Book Topics* or *Braille Book Review*, bimonthly magazines that list all the new books. *Talking Book Topics* lists cassette and disc books; *Braille Book Review* lists braille books. Both magazines include a brief description of the book, the author, narrator, accession number, and the number of records or cassettes which make up that complete book. Any strong language, explicit descriptions of sex, and controversial subjects are also noted. Each of these magazines is divided: type of media; adult and juvenile; and fiction and nonfiction. Order forms included for users to indicate the books they would like to read are returned, postage free, to the cooperating library. *Talking Book Topics* is available in flexible disc, large print, and cassette, with an order blank in braille. *Braille Book Review* comes in large print and braille. Every two years a cumulative edition is published for each media (disc, cassette, and braille) consisting of the books that appeared in *Talking Book Topics* or *Braille Book Review* during that period.

Eligible readers can request a disc machine, a cassette machine, or both. Machines issued through the Library of Congress program must be used since talking books are recorded at a slower speed than commercial materials. Talking book records are recorded at 8 rpm (revolutions per minute) rather than 33 ⅓ rpm; talking book cassettes are recorded at 15/16 ips (inches per second) rather than the standard cassette speed of 1 7/8 ips. This enables NLS to get more on each record or cassette, and the reader does not have to change the record or cassette so often. Cassette books have the added advantage of being 4-track instead of the standard 2-track cassettes. Readers listen to side one, turn the cassette over and listen to side two, then push a side selector switch located on the cassette player and turn the cassette back over to listen to side three, and again turn the cassette over to listen to side four. Therefore, cassette books, besides being played at half the speed of commercial cassettes, also have two additional tracks, providing four times as much recorded material on an NLS cassette as a commercial cassette. A typical Agatha Christie mystery could be recorded on a single NLS cassette, and would consist of approximately six hours listening.

Cassette books were added to the NLS program on an experimental basis in the early 1970s and have become so popular that by 1981 all fiction and nonfiction books will be on cassette tapes while all bestsellers and magazines will be in another new format called flexible disc. Flexible discs are a thin synthetic material which are much cheaper to produce than the familiar rigid discs, though they lack durability. Bestsellers and magazines are ideal for this media since they are more ephemeral. Because of their low production cost, many more copies of titles can be made available on flexible discs than rigid discs. Like paperback books, it is only intended that several circulations be received from each copy of the flexible discs before they are discarded. For more permanent copies, books are produced on cassette tapes in addition to the less durable flexible discs. Flexible disc editions are generally produced several months before the cassette editions in order to have materials reach the users who are primarily interested in the immediacy of their reading material. Reissues of classics, which a large number of people enjoy rereading, are also produced as flexible discs. These include such things as Laura Ingalls Wilder's "Little House" series, Lewis Carroll's *Alice in Wonderland*, and Frank Baum's *Wizard of Oz*.

Cassette and disc books are designed to make them as easy as possible for a blind or physically handicapped reader to use. On discs, the odd side of the label is in braille, the even side in large print, so even if readers do not know braille they can tell which side of the record they are placing on the turntable. Cassettes combine a braille and print label on the odd side and leave the even side blank. Instructions are narrated at the end of each side of the recording telling the reader how to proceed, for example, "end of side 1, to continue turn the disc over" or "end of side 2, to continue change side selector switch and turn the cassette over." Even so, many readers become confused over cassettes numbered 1, 5, 9, and so on, thinking they are missing sides when, in fact, these are the four-sided cassettes with sides 1, 2, 3, and 4 all on one cassette. Cassettes are numbered according to the first side on that cassette. Older people and those with a mental impairment often find the discs easier to use because of this.

Twin vision or print/braille books are another popular format for children. These are conventional print books with braille overlays that are used to help parents, teachers, and children learn together. Twin vision books enable a blind parent and a sighted child or a sighted parent and a blind child to read together. Many popular titles are produced in this format including the Dr. Seuss favorites. Sharing with a blind or handicapped child is just as important as sharing with a sighted or nonhandicapped child. It is important to create an atmosphere early in the child's life that reinforces the idea that although the child is handicapped, he or she can lead a normal life.

Talking Book Machines and Attachments

Talking book machines are designed to make them as simple as possible to use while still offering a clear tone and several special features to aid readers, although some critics claim the machines could be made even simpler. Disc machines operate in a similar manner to commercially available phonograph machines. An extra speed for the 8 rpm records; volume, tone, on-off, and so on noted in braille as well as print; and an automatic cutoff are the major differences between an NLS machine and a regular phonograph. The automatic cutoff was designed to make the disc player easier to use. When the record ends, the tone arm activates a stop swtich which cuts off the power to the machine so the talking book machine motor is not left running. Special tabs that help the reader place the discs on the machine can be flipped back out of the way when the reader wishes to play the larger 33⅓ rpm commercial discs. Another guide helps the user place the tone arm at the beginning of the record, and a detachable hood can be used as a separate speaker. Needles are two sided, and by flipping, an easily located lever next to the needle places the new side of the needle into playing position. Replacement cartridges are available free of charge through cooperating libraries.

Cassette machines have the added advantage of also having a battery pack which plays for about eight hours before it needs to be recharged. It is suggested that the machine be left plugged in so it is charged and ready to go when the user has need of it. "Eject," "rewind," "play," "fast forward," and "stop" are marked with tactile symbols rather than braille. Cassette machines have a variable speed control which can slow down or speed up the narrator's voice. Some hearing impaired persons have difficulty understanding the narrator and slowing down the voice lowers it to a more audible pitch. The speed can be increased to play so fast that the narrator's voice is totally distorted. An attachment available for purchase from several commercial sources alleviates this "Donald Duck" effect, but is not offered as one of the free attachments on the NLS program. A speech selector switch enables the reader to play commercially produced 1 7/8 ips cassettes as well as the 15/16 ips cassettes produced by NLS. Four-track tapes are played by depressing the side selector switch to the required track. Commercial cassettes can be played by leaving the side selector switch in the "1-2" position. Cassette players also have an automatic cutoff that turns off the power should the reader forget to press the "stop" switch when the side is completed. Cassette players are just that—players. They do not record, although the American Printing House for the Blind in Louisville, Kentucky, produces a cassette player/recorder for purchase which plays the 15/16 ips NLS cassettes.

Instructions for operation and maintenance are included in braille, large print, and/or disc or cassette for each machine mailed out. Readers are strongly encouraged to read thoroughly these instructions to become familiar with the operation of the machines and use of the materials. Blind or visually impaired persons often need the assistance of a sighted person, because if they do not read braille (and most blind people do not) or see well enough to read large print, they cannot turn on the machine to listen to the instructions. Teachers can keep their handicapped students interested and enthusiastic about reading by showing an interest in helping them learn to work their machines and select books. Students should be made to feel "special" and not "different" because they use recorded materials.

Several attachments are available for use with the equipment, free of charge, through the NLS program.

TONE ARM CLIP. The tone arm clip is a plastic hook shaped into an "L" which is clipped onto the tone arm of the talking book machine and used to assist physically handicapped patrons in placing the tone arm on the record. Tone arm clips are positioned on the tone arm by the library before the machine is mailed out to users.

HEADPHONES. A jack located on the front of the disc machine and the side of the cassette machine fits a standard headset available in any radio or music store. NLS also issues headphones which are similar to any available commercially, featuring a volume control for each ear. There is also a switch marked "amplifier" which can be placed in the "on" position to use that attachment. Headphones are useful for the hard of hearing and handicapped students in a classroom or study hall situation.

AMPLIFIER. The amplifer is the newest and most controversial of NLS's attachments, and a special application must be completed in order to receive it. This attachment plugs into the headphone jack on both the disc and cassette player, and the headphone, in turn, plugs into the amplifier. Extreme caution must be practiced in utilizing the amplifier since someone with normal hearing could have their hearing permanently impaired should they use the headphones when the amplifier is plugged in. Because it magnifies sound to the equivalent of a large airplane in full throttle, the potential for great harm is present, yet the needs of the hearing impaired must counterbalance this. NLS has been involved in lengthy litigation to determine the best ways to protect both themselves and their users, and has concluded that all amplifiers would be distributed directly by NLS, rather than the regional libraries, and only upon receipt of the user's special application properly completed.

Many have asked why, if the amplifier is so potentially dangerous, it is being produced at all. This question is best answered by describing several of the people who use it. Joe has had brain tumors since he was fourteen. He is now twenty-nine and within four credit hours of receiving his bachelor's degree. He is nearly totally blind, his balance seriously impaired, and he woke up one day from a nap almost totally deaf from the pressure of a tumor on his eardrums. An operation was able to restore part of his hearing, but not enough to enable him to listen to talking books without the volume turned all the way up. Listening to talking books is the major way Joe spends his days, and the amplifier makes it easier and more comfortable for him. Mrs. Carlton is ninety-two years old and has been a talking book patron for years. Recently her hearing became so bad that she could no longer listen to the talking books, her major source of entertainment and information. With the amplifier, she can once again enjoy talking books. These two examples best illustrates the case for the amplifier. Conversely, the danger always exists of a child coming into the room, placing on the headphones and turning the machine on with the amplifier plugged in, and perhaps permanently damaging his or her hearing. Responsibility must ultimately rest with the user to assure the proper use of the equipment.

The amplifier is, by no means, the answer for everyone with a hearing loss accompanied by a visual and/or physical problem. Some types of hearing problems do not respond to sound amplification and someone who is only slightly hard of hearing should certainly not apply for this attachment. The amplifier is indisputably beneficial, but the potential for harm must also be realized and safeguarded against.

PILLOWPHONE. The pillowphone is used by readers confined to bed and is often used in place of a headphone. It plugs into the same jack utilized with the headphone. As the name suggests, the pillowphone lies on the pillow next to the person's ear and localizes the noise so it does not disturb other people. Paraplegics confined to their beds have found the pillowphone a successful alternative to headphones.

All this equipment is available through regional libraries throughout the United States and is issued upon receipt of a properly certified application for talking book library service. Several states have established machine lending agencies separate from the library whose sole responsibility is the distribution and maintenance of the talking book machines, although the majority of libraries combine the library and machine service. Talking book machines are federal property and are issued on loan as long as the reader uses the service—they are not given to readers. Only one stipulation exists for using the talking books: once a year a reader borrows and returns a book. If this requirement is not met, the machines are subject to recall. Many readers have the idea the machine is theirs for life. This is not true. Machines are loaned to patrons *only* while they are using the service. Machines are not to be resold, given to friends, or in any way damaged or abused. One user actually left her talking book machine to a niece in her will, which was, of course, strictly illegal.

NLS is always working to improve their machines and attachments. A prototype for a combination talking book and cassette machine has been developed and may be added to the program in several years. Automatic tracking is a special feature of this machine. This means that once the cassette is placed in the machine it can be played in its entirety without having to turn it over at the end of each side. Therefore, a reader can listen for an uninterrupted six hours without removing the cassette from the machine. The combination machine has all the capabilities of the current disc and cassette machines including automatic cutoff, variable speed control, and battery pack. The machine weighs fourteen pounds, slightly more than the present disc machine, and would also be issued free of charge to eligible readers.

Another prototype being developed is a simplified cassette machine which would fit into a pocket, making it especially practical for students. Although it would have fewer controls than the present cassette player, its compactness and portability would make up for any lack of special features. Automatic tracking would be another feature of this simplified machine. NLS would still continue to offer the regular cassette player currently used.

Since cassettes are now a major part of the NLS program, several important changes will be made in the future. Leader tape, the colored cellophane at the beginning and end of each tape, is being adapted to have a cleaning substance which would pass over the heads of the cassette machine and prevent a carbon buildup. New packaging is being experimented with which would make containers easier to open and smaller. NLS is continually striving to make its materials more efficient and easy to use. One of its most recent projects is "fast indexing." In 1979, *Access National Parks* was issued, the first NLS book to utilize fast indexing. When placed in the "fast forward" speed, chapter titles are read and the user stops the machine at the desired chapter. By pressing the "stop" button, then the "play" button, the reader is at the beginning of that chapter. Fast indexing makes a cassette dictionary possible for the first time, since before it would have been necessary to hit the "stop" and "play" button until the user stumbled across the word for which he or she was searching. Fast indexing can be used on anthologies and other collections of this type, making it faster and more convenient for the user to get access to the needed material.

Braille and Large Print Materials

Braille is the least used of media. It is bulky and hard to handle, and is the least popular among readers. *Gone With the Wind* in braille consists of twelve volumes, not something one would easily carry along to read during lunch! Problems in size also create problems in shipping for the libraries and post office. Braille books are packed into three or four cartons and mailed off to teachers, often to the chagrin of postal workers on walking routes. But, in spite of these drawbacks, braille still plays an important part in communication for the blind and visually impaired that must not be underestimated. Students and workers are always going to need some way to take notes, whether for class or work, and to be able to refer back to what they have done, whether it be to study for a test or write an annual report.

The use of braille may receive new life from a technological advance which can place braille on standard cassette tapes. These tapes are inserted into a specially designed player with a series of pins that raise and lower to form braille cells as the cassette tape passes through. Cassette braille, sometimes called electronic braille or paperless braille, utilizes the audiocassette machine with several major differences. According to a research report produced by NLS the distinctions are: braille input is accomplished by using braille writer keys; electronic signals on the cassette tape represent braille characters instead of voice or music; and the output is in braille. A student would conceivably take the cassette-braille machine to class, take notes directly on the cassette tape by using the braille keyboard, and later be able to refer back to the notes by use of the display pins at the top surface of the machine.

Three prototypes of the cassette-braille machine are now being evaluated and field tested by NLS. Several factors must be taken into account before the machine is offered as a standard part of the program. These include acceptance by braille readers of this method of reading, refinement of preferred features, and unit cost. It is almost universally agreed that cassette-braille would drastically lower the cost of producing braille. Conventional press braille costs an average of $33.00 per book copy; hand-copied braille an average of $50.00 a copy. Multiply these costs by the number of braille books NLS produces yearly on a national basis and the results are staggering. Cassette braille would lower the amount needed to produce one copy to $5.00 and have the added advantage of being compact and easily portable. With the high cost of producing standard Grade II braille, even a cassette-braille machine costing over $1,000 would be a saving in the long run.

Disc, cassette, and braille books are the media produced by NLS. Many cooperating libraries supplement these with large print materials. Any type size over sixteen point is considered large print and no special certification is required to use these books and magazines. Several publishers, such as G. K. Hall, have special divisions producing large print. Many teachers needing large print materials find it impossible to obtain them, and looking through catalogs of large print publishers for elementary materials is a waste of time and effort since these companies largely produce adult books. Some juvenile books, especially at the kindergarten through third grade level, already qualify as large print since they use such a large point size. Many publishers now print the point sizes in their juvenile catalogs and these are the best sources for large print juvenile materials. *Large Print Books in Print* also lists various large print publishers in the back of the volume.

Library service to the handicapped requires that talking book libraries do more than just distribute NLS materials. They must be a source of other types of information. A good regional or sub-regional library should be a place where patrons are made to feel they are individuals, not reader statistics.

Reference Services for the Blind and Physically Handicapped

Because of the limited number of materials available, reference service plays a major part in any regional library and materials must be utilized to their utmost. Giving reference service to the handicapped presents an additional challenge because, not only must the information be located, it must also be placed into a format the patron can use. Many times the latter problem is the more difficult since it involves recording material or converting it into braille or large print. Besides answering the standard reference questions that public libraries receive, these libraries receive many inquiries such as, how to obtain a special handicapped parking decal; how to go about getting a guide dog; where to purchase a table top magnifier; and what special education options are available to children. Libraries serving the handicapped become the local place that people turn to, not only for information, but referral as well. Regional libraries become the contact point for a myriad of other agencies offering service to the handicapped including rehabilitation agencies, special schools, and state institutions.

"Reader advisor" is a term in common use among the NLS network libraries in conjunction with reference services. In its broadest sense, a reader advisor is a person who is familiar with books, as well as information available through the NLS program and resources available outside the program. Because of the specialized knowledge that is necessary, a reader advisor should be a professional librarian. Reader advisors are responsible for the selection of materials sent to users, maintenance of reader files, and communicating with the patrons. They research special requests, contact related agencies, and distribute appropriate materials. Their role is unique and their philosophy must be to give complete service to users. If patrons are for some reason unable to select the books they would like to read from *Talking Books Topics* or *Braille Book Review*, reader advisors are responsible for selecting reading materials.

If the information requested cannot be found locally, requests are forwarded to the NLS reference section which processes some 10,000 requests each year ranging from simple queries on the availability of a bestseller to requests for subject bibliographies. NLS will notify librarians of the status of a particular title, that is, if it is being considered for production, is in the process of being produced, or will be sent soon. Recently NLS put its microfiche catalog into the Bibliographic Retrieval System (BRS) data base to do on-line searches. Regional libraries with automated circulation systems also have the capability of using the BRS data base system which makes subject searching fast and simple. For example, the computer can do a data base search for all romances that have been narrated by men in a matter of minutes. A list of these books and their accession numbers is sent to the requesting library and noted in the patron's folder.

Services of Volunteers

If materials cannot be obtained through NLS, volunteers in regional and subregional libraries can record on cassettes or braille the desired information available only in print. Special materials such as information for a school report or items of local interest can only be accessed at the local level, making obvious the need for having production capability within the regional library system.

Many items to which able-bodied library users have access still are not available to handicapped users, making utilization of all available materials essential. Last year NLS produced approximately 1,600 recorded titles and 360 braille titles at a cost of $27 million dollars. This may seem like a large number of titles, but when compared to the quantity of print titles produced commercially each year, it is very minimal. Volunteers can make a viable contribution to expanding this base collection of materials through regional recording programs. NLS's talking book collection is designed for a general audience, that is, patrons from all across the United States, and not to a specific local audience. Regional libraries fill this gap by recording materials not available on the national program. These may range from materials which are included in a local collection development plant to special requests by readers. Local recording programs may not have the same high quality of narrated NLS books but need of the material many times overrides the need for quality to many readers. This is not to say local libraries should not be continually striving to improve their product. Excellence should always be an aim. Several regional libraries produce recorded books that rival those produced by NLS and, indeed, are sometimes included among those which NLS distributes.

Raising funds for recording booths and equipment is an ideal volunteer undertaking. Many states run their local recording programs entirely on volunteer funds and time. These locally recorded books are available to other regional libraries through interlibrary loan. Master copies are sent to the requesting library, which can duplicate them for its collection; the master tape is returned to the issuing library. Interlibrary loan and local recording programs help to broaden the base of available materials.

Persons who cannot read conventional print do not have the

option of going to their local bookstore and purchasing the print copy of a book if the library does not have it. If the talking book library cannot supply the book, they have no other source. Local recording programs fill this need for material by utilizing their own resources.

Besides narrating and monitoring books, volunteers can help supplement the services offered by the staff. Libraries use volunteers to deliver machines to new readers and demonstrate how they work; call new readers and explain library procedures and whom to contact in case of a problem; and continue contact with users who sometimes just want someone to talk to. Volunteers can also help with many office procedures such as stamping brochures and checking books for completeness.

Telephone Pioneers of America is the best-known volunteer group working in conjunction with the talking book library program. To be a telephone pioneer, a person must have worked in the telephone industry, (AT&T, ITT, or the Bell System) for at least eighteen years. Telephone pioneers repair broken talking book machines, cassette machines, and braillers and often make pickup and delivery of equipment to the user's home. Special training aids are available through NLS to help train telephone pioneers. All necessary repair parts are sent from NLS to facilitate the pioneers in their work. Often regional libraries have a technician who works with the telephone pioneers and helps coordinate their efforts.

Besides the repair program, telephone pioneers have developed many learning aids which are used by the blind and deaf. These include beeping Easter eggs, baseballs, and basketballs that blind children can use to participate in sports similar to their sighted contemporaries. Many toys developed by the telephone pioneers to aid teachers working with deaf children have been an outstanding success. Best known of these toys is the climbing squirrel, Scamper, developed by Mississippi's telephone pioneers. Scamper utilizes amplifiers found on telephone receivers. When a person speaks into the receiver attached to Scamper, the amplifier transmits the voice impulses through a relay to activate the motor, causing the squirrel to climb the tree. When the voice stops, Scamper goes back to the base of the tree. This allows deaf children to see the results of their voices even if they cannot hear any sound. Scamper is also used with emotionally disturbed children who do not speak. The action of the squirrel stimulates emotionally disturbed children to want to make sounds.

Specially designed toy dolls, tigers, and race tracks are other aids to encourage speech that were developed by pioneers. Both the tiger and the doll have eyes that light up when someone speaks into the receivers. Two cars and two receivers on the race track allow children to compete. The more the children speak, the faster and farther the cars move, encouraging children to make a continuous flow of speech. A voice activated toy train operates in a similar fashion.

From parts of old pinball machines, pioneers have built Elcode machines to aid in teaching the handicapped. Used mainly with cerebral palsied children, the Elcode aids teachers in communicating with students who cannot speak or who have little muscular control. The machine consists of a board with panels and a set of interchangeable cards. Each label has a light that lights up in sequence. After setting up the cards, the teacher begins a lighting sequence by remote control. Students give answers to the teacher's questions by stopping the lights at the correct card using another remote control.

The role pioneers play in assisting regional libraries is more than just one of repairing broken equipment. Their efforts greatly expand the scope of services regional libraries are able to offer and their continued innovations create new learning and living experiences for the blind and deaf.

Many regional libraries have friends groups, besides their pioneers, to assist them in meeting the goals of their library service. One of the major needs Friends of Libraries fill is fund raising. Talking book programs and local recording programs are expensive and much of the funding to expand programs must come from outside sources. Friends have helped purchase recording booths, recording equipment, blank tapes, empty containers for talking books, and a variety of other materials that the library would not be able to afford by itself. Most friends groups are incorporated as nonprofit, tax-exempt organizations so all contributions are tax deductible. Local businesses, churches, and civic clubs are encouraged to contribute. Many parents of handicapped children are eager to get involved with friends groups since this organization is a means of involving themselves in a civic service which also assists their children.

Many regional libraries utilize the volunteer services of a task force composed of users of the service and professionals in the field who help plan the service's goals and objectives for the coming year. A teacher, librarian, and parent are included in this group to express the needs of the educational sector. No regional library is truly meeting the needs of their readers unless they have a user group which has input into the service and can accomplish improvements through valid criticisms.

Textbook Services

Besides basic library services available to regional libraries through the NLS program, organizations exist which supplement these available materials. Many regional libraries also act as contact points for these services, the best known of which is Recording for the Blind.

Recording for the Blind (RFB) is the major source of textbooks available on open reel and cassette tapes. Virtually any textbook a student needs is obtainable from this source. RFB is a nonprofit national organization utilizing over 5,000 trained volunteers who work in twenty-nine professionally equipped recording studios located throughout the United States. Readers eligible for the NLS talking book library program are also eligible for RFB. There are several major differences, however. RFB services are provided exclusively on an individual basis; institutions such as schools cannot sign up as borrowers. Borrowers are signed up for RFB for life. Nor are machines included on the RFB program although RFB's recorded textbooks are compatible to the NLS equipment.

RFB serves users of all ages from kindergarten through the professional level. Many students have completed school, including college, using this service and continue using it as professionals to keep up to date in their fields. RFB's services are made possible through voluntary contributions from corporations, foundations, and individuals. Each new book recorded represents a total investment of over $100.

A special application must be completed to register for the service. Pertinent information on the user's needs is to be given on one side, while the other side is a disability statement which must be completed and signed by a qualified professional person, that is, a doctor, nurse, or counselor. Like the NLS application, those with reading disabilities must be certified by a medical doctor and all information is confidential.

A second sheet, a "Request for Recorded Books," must also be completed, listing the textbooks the reader needs. Detailed information is required as to author, title, publisher, date, and edition. RFB produces a catalog listing available textbooks. If the reader does not wish to purchase this catalog, many regional libraries will fill in these numbers for the user if the form is returned to them. Readers need to check before returning RFB forms to regional libraries to ascertain if their regional library is one which acts as a liaison for RFB. Many regional libraries with a large number of readers do not have the staff to provide this service.

If the needed textbook is not in the catalog, users should give RFB as much bibliographic information as possible. Since new titles are always being recorded, not all available titles are listed. Readers are notified if the title has not been produced. They can then supply RFB with two print copies of the needed book (which are returned upon completion), and RFB will record the materials for the reader.

Master topics of recorded textbooks are retrieved and duplicated when requests are received. Acknowledgment slips denoting the status of the textbooks are sent on receipt of all orders. A blank request form for the next order is sent with all acknowledgments. Although student orders are given priority over other requests, students should order books well in advance of when they will be needed. RFB has the capacity to fill 1,000 orders a day, but in September and before new semesters start, they receive nearly twice this number. During the rest of the year, requests are filled in two to three weeks but in these busy periods the time lag is much greater.

All RFB textbooks are loaned for a one year period to allow the student to have use of them for the entire school year. Textbooks utilize a sound indexing system where a single beep is superimposed over each page announcement. Double tones are used to denote the beginnings of chapters, sections, and divisions of the book. These tones are only audible in the "fast forward" and "rewind" modes of the cassette machines. Raised line drawings are included when appropriate, particularly in books on mathematics and the sciences, aiding the students in using graphs and figures. Users can indicate if they have an interest in these special tactile drawings when ordering books.

RFB is a source for textbooks of which all teachers should be aware, since in most states the education department is only required to supply large print textbooks and no other format. For students who are blind, physically handicapped, or reading disabled, large print textbooks provide no aid at all and teachers must turn to outside sources to fulfill the needs of their students. Many educators, even special education teachers, are unaware of the existence of these resources so an important source of materials remains untapped. Students first learn of the availability of these services through the school system and even if they do not utilize the available materials it is important that they at least be aware of the services to which they are entitled. Of the many services available, the majority are entirely free of charge, and an extra unnecessary burden is placed upon students when they do not avail themselves of these special services.

Another textbook service is made available through the Instructional Materials Reference Center for Visually Handicapped Children, a division of the American Printing House for the Blind (APH). Available books are listed in its *Central Catalog*. APH's *Central Catalog* began in the early 1960s as a list of hand-transcribed braille textbooks available for loan or reproduction and has expanded in its eleventh edition to two volumes the size of a large city phone directory. Materials listed are primarily school textbooks available in braille, tapes (both open reel and cassette), and large print produced by volunteer and commercial companies. Entries are photocopied from a card file updated daily. If a textbook is not in the *Central Catalog*, queries can be directed to APH, who will refer to the file to ascertain if the book has been produced since the catalog went to press.

Textbooks are listed alphabetically by title. These titles are not necessarily available through APH; the *Central Catalog* is intended as a source directory of available materials, *not* a supplier. Each entry includes the title, author, publisher, format, and source of each edition. If a master (braille) is one produced by APH, a thermoform copy can be made and charged to the federal quota account, in the case of public schools, or ordered on an accounts receivable basis.

In addition to its catalog, APH produces a number of bibliographies of materials available for purchase in braille, large type, and recorded formats. These bibliographies are kept on file for use by interested readers in regional and subregional talking book libraries and include a number of popular fiction and nonfiction titles as well as textbooks.

The National Braille Association's *Braille Book Bank Catalog* is an important source of textbooks in braille for high school and college courses. Many special education divisions of state departments of education do not provide textbooks at the junior college or university level and the job of finding textbooks in a usable format is left to the teacher and student. If the student is a client of a rehabilitation agency, the agency often pays for the textbook. The expense must otherwise be borne by the student unless the college has made special arrangements. Of course, Recording for the Blind provides free textbooks on cassette, but the Braille Book Bank is of great assistance in supplying braille textbooks, even though there is a charge for the materials. All braille books are prepared by volunteers and offered at less than cost. Students sometimes prefer using braille textbooks, especially when charts and graphs are involved, because the use of line drawings makes comprehension of these charts clearer.

All braillists doing the transcribing are certified by the Library of Congress and their hand-transcribed braille masters are thermoformed for distribution. The collection of the Braille Book Bank is listed in three catalogs (music, textbooks, and general interest materials) which are available free of charge in print or braille upon request. Again, student orders are given priority. Another service of the National Braille Association is the Braille Technical Tables Bank, which provides thermoform copies of over 300 hand-transcribed technical, mathematical, and scientific tables.

Numerous other organizations with similar services exist, providing textbooks in large print, braille, and recorded formats. With the exception of the NLS program and the Recording for the Blind program, the majority of these sources charge a fee for their materials. Two that provide materials produced to order are Volunteer Services for the Blind and Volunteer Transcribing Services. Teachers must plan ahead to determine which formats are to be used by their students and where the materials can be obtained. If the materials must be purchased, it may be necessary to request them from the state department of education. Under Public Law 94-142, states are now required to provide an IEP and the materials necessary for the student to function successfully within that program.

Special Aids and Equipment

Special aids besides textbooks are sometimes necessary. The American Foundation for the Blind in New York offers the most comprehensive catalog of aids available to the blind and visually impaired ranging from beeping basketballs to large print crossword puzzles. Their catalogs are available free of charge in large print, braille, and cassette. Other aids, such as special games, globes, and tactile kits are available from the APH in Louisville, Kentucky. APH and Telesensory Systems in Palo Alto, California offer the "Speech +" calculator which enables visually impaired students the convenience and accuracy of conventional models. This talking calculator verbally verifies all keystrokes and has a twenty-four word vocabulary. Besides the capability of completing standard mathematics, the calculator features an independent memory, floating decimal point, change of sign key, and algebraic logic. Priced at about $400, the calculator can be hand-held and has a rechargeable battery. Volume can be raised or lowered and an earphone may be used if desired.

Some school systems have purchased a video low-vision aid utilizing a television monitor, camera, and lens. Best known of these are two models sold under the brand names, "Visualtek" and "Apollo." Regular print books are placed under the camera and the enlarged image appears on the television screen. Many teachers have found this aid a quick answer for students who need large print. A major disadvantage is that the system is not easily portable and must usually remain in one location, sometimes making access difficult. However, in the proper school setting, such as a media center, the Visualtek and Apollo can give access to print books that visually handicapped students might not ordinarily be able to use. Various models are available, ranging from some which are simple in design and serve the same function as tabletop magnifiers to sophisticated models utilizing typewriters and several cameras. Prices vary accordingly, but the standard system currently costs approximately $2,200. High school teachers in particular may want to consider the purchase of a Visualtek or Apollo to aid their students in completing research papers where access to a number of books is necessary.

Another aid coming into increased use is the *Optacon* developed by Telesensory Systems, Inc. (TSI). The Optacon (OPtical-to-TActile CONverter) converts regular ink print into a readable vibrating tactile form through a series of 144 vibrating pins which rise and fall as a camera passes over the printed word. Small and portable, the Optacon gives blind users immediate access to the printed word. Different type styles and languages can be read because the pins reproduce exactly what the camera sees. Weighing only four pounds, the Optacon is a battery operated unit, the size of a small cassette player, that consists of three parts, the camera, the electronics section, and the tactile stimulator. The miniature camera is moved across the printed page, sending electronic impulses to the pins (tactile stimulator) to form the original image that a blind person can feel with one finger. Blind users thus have the same access to the printed word as sighted readers, enabling them to read print textbooks, correspondence, bank statements, and a myriad of other items sighted readers take for granted. Easily adapted, the Optacon can be used by blind computer operators to read cathode-ray tube terminals or by blind typists to read what is being typed and fill out preprinted forms. Each unit costs approximately $2,900, and special attachments and lenses are available.

Training is essential to use the Optacon and TSI offers various courses across the country for new users as well as special courses for both the blind and the sighted who want to be certified to teach the use of the Optacon. Many readers have had their lives greatly expanded by utilizing the Optacon. They not only have access to many more materials, but are also able to find employment in jobs that their inability to use conventional print formerly prevented them from holding. Other readers have found the Optacon slow and difficult to use. Individual preference seems to determine how successful readers are in using the Optacon. Many public schools are now training their eligible junior and senior high school age students in its use and encouraging teachers to prepare materials so students become proficient in working with the machine.

A much more expensive machine that converts print into a format usable by the blind is the Kurzweil Reading Machine (KRM). Initially conceived in 1966, the KRM may someday allow immediate access to the printed word, making talking books obsolete. Slightly larger than a tabletop photocopier, the KRM converts books, magazines, letters, and almost any other printed material into spoken English. The material to be read is placed face down on the glass surface of the scanner and when the control unit is activated, a scanning mechanism automatically locates the first line of the text and an electronic voice begins reading the material. Different Reading functions can be performed according to the needs of the user through the use of thirty-three controls. At the simplest level, the reading rate can be decreased or increased; the machine can be asked to spell words; and the KRM can repeat the previous few lines. Ten hours of training are necessary to learn to use its controls and fully utilize all its capabilities. The KRM is programmed to decide how to pronounce words. It has been "taught" over 1,000 linguistic rules and 2,500 exceptions. Since the KRM uses synthetic speech it is sometimes hard to understand, although the more a user works with the machine, the easier it is to comprehend. Each subsequent model of the KRM improves the speech capability to make the voice sound more human. New models are being taught to emphasize certain words so the text is not read in a monotone.

Kurzweil's first model cost $50,000, and the current model costs $23,000, a substantial drop in cost, although the price is still prohibitive for individual purchase. Every state now has at least one model of the KRM available for demonstration and use. These are located primarily in schools, libraries, and rehabilitation agencies. Although the KRM cannot read everything, new programs are continually being developed to expand its range. A hand tracking option now makes it possible to scan a page to get a mental image of the layout. Readers can switch back and forth between manual and automatic tracking if they desire. By changing the program tape cartridge, the KRM can be converted into a talking calculator capable of all scientific functions. Basic programming language is fed into the calculator allowing users to solve complicated problems. Another attachment being developed under contract with NLS allows the machine to translate printed material into Grade 2 braille. The KRM also reads the English text from computers and CRT terminals, making it capable of performing a variety of functions.

Both the Optacon and the Kurzweil are the wave of the future and over the next ten years will revolutionize the opportunities available to the blind and visually impaired. Total access to all materials in print is now within the foreseeable future and may radically alter the lives of millions of blind citizens.

The Role of Teachers and Librarians

Mainstreaming a handicapped child into a classroom is not a simple thing for teachers who are not experienced in special education, yet the number of aids and information available to assist the handicapped helps make the job easier. Responsibility still rests with the teacher and parent to take full advantage of these materials and to utilize them in the most constructive manner. Further responsibility rests upon the teacher to make the child and the special books or equipment acceptable to the other children in the classroom. Handicapped students are often rejected by their peers because of the lack of understanding of what causes a handicap and the nature of it. Educating able-bodied students to the problems of their handicapped classmates is an important part of mainstreaming. Teachers may choose to do this by incorporating studies of various handicaps with biology or other science courses or assigning papers on braille and other forms of communication.

Demonstrating talking books and talking book equipment illustrates to students that learning is done by listening as well as reading.

School library collections should include print books on persons with handicaps to educate sighted and able-bodied students. Everyone has some type of handicap such as a fear of the dark or of heights. The handicaps most people have are not visible. Children, as well as adults, should learn to associate with and accept people who are different from themselves. School libraries can help by including stories in both print and recorded formats about famous people who had handicaps such as Helen Keller, Franklin Roosevelt, and Ludwig van Beethoven, emphasizing their talents rather than their disabilities. Numerous titles for juveniles have been produced over the last several years dealing with children with handicaps. These include *Shelley's Day* by Candance Catlin Hall, a pictorial story of a day in the life of a visually handicapped child; and *Me and Einstein* by Rose Blue, a fictional story of a child with a reading disability. Story hours should be planned by librarians to include the disabled and to draw handicapped children into story participation. With visually impaired children this might include using a juvenile story in large print format with colorful illustrations. For older children, book discussions might include a novel concerning a child with a handicap.

Librarians working with blind or handicapped children should determine what materials their students need. Can they use large print or are recorded or braille materials necessary? Are there sufficient titles in the needed media? If the library is not capable of meeting these needs they must turn to outside sources such as the National Library Service for the Blind and Physically Handicapped and the American Printing House for the Blind for necessary materials. Reference materials are also available in special formats, for example, both the *World Book Encyclopedia* and *Webster's Dictionary* can be purchased in both large type and braille formats. Books and periodicals concerning special education should be included in the library's professional collection. Many teachers who are now having handicapped children mainstreamed into their classrooms have little or no special education training and these professional materials can be of great assistance. Articles dealing with the integration of handicapped children into regular classrooms and the curricular methods used can now be found in great detail in most professional journals. The American Foundation for the Blind produces an excellent brochure available free of charge entitled *When You Have a Visually Handicapped Child in Your Classroom: Suggestions for Teachers.*

Disabled children have the same reading interests as their sighted, able-bodied classmates. They like mysteries, stories about space, animals, and adventure. They have the same likes and dislikes as any child and the school library's collection of materials in special formats should be comprehensive enough to meet these needs. Librarians planning book discussions and research projects should bear this in mind and allow the child to choose the subject that interests him or her rather than to choose a topic the teacher feels is appropriate for a disabled child to study. A great temptation exists for teachers and librarians to overprotect handicapped students. As much as possible, disabled students should be treated like others in the classroom. Ruth Velleman, in her book *Serving Physically Disabled People*, includes a list of guidelines for librarians dealing with handicapped users that can be used by any person dealing with the disabled:

1. Offer assistance as you would to anyone else, for example, to push a wheelchair or to guide a blind person. The person will indicate whether or not the help is needed, and a "no, thank you" must be respected.
2. Noticing an obvious disability is not rude; however, asking personal questions about it is inappropriate.
3. Always talk directly to a disabled person rather than to the person who may be accompanying him or her. Never talk about a disabled person to the person he or she is with as if the person did not exist.
4. Do not be concerned if you use the words "talking" or "running" when talking to a person in a wheelchair, or "Do you see?" when talking to a blind person. Disabled people use these words themselves and think nothing of it.

5. Do not avoid using words like blind or deaf when associating with people with these disabilities. Disabled people know that they are disabled and do not need to be shielded from the facts.
6. When talking with a person in a wheelchair for any length of time it is better to sit down in order to be at the same eye level.
7. Be sensitive to architectural barriers in your libraries.
8. Remember that if a person does not turn around in response to a call, it may be that he or she is deaf. A light tap on the shoulder to get a person's attention makes sense.
9. Never gesture about a blind person to someone else who may be present. This will inevitably be picked up on and make the person who is blind feel that you are talking behind his or her back.
10. Lip reading by deaf persons can be aided by being sure that the light is on your face and not behind you, and by taking all obstructions such as pipes, cigarettes, or gum out of the mouth, keeping the lips flexible, and speaking slowly. Additional communication could include body language, pantomime and gestures of all kinds, and written communication if necessary.

In short, a handicapped person, whether adult or child, should be treated with the same respect and awareness of their rights that is accorded an able-bodied person.

Teachers and librarians can help by providing the materials and support necessary for the disabled to receive an equal education. Obtaining materials from NLS, RFB, APH, and other sources is only a small part of providing an educational program for a disabled child. Talking books are a tool; teachers and libraries are the key to their use and utilization. Attitudes toward disabled students are reflected in their attitudes toward themselves. If a teacher treats a child as an inconvenient burden, other students in the class and the child himself reflect this opinion. Unfortunately, some teachers do have this attitude. If so, parents may then turn to advocacy groups or other organizations founded to insure the rights of their clients to secure an independent education program that is suitable for their child.

Library service to the handicapped, whether at the public or
school level, should not be an extra frill or "special" service the
library offers. The disabled have the same right and privilege to
read as any citizen and should have the same materials available to
them. The satisfaction that any reader has with library service
depends on how adequately his or her needs are met by available
materials. The same standards of service must be applicable to both
the handicapped and able-bodied. Not only is this philosophy the
right of every individual, it is now a law.

Conclusion

Responsibility for implementing an effective independent education program rests with the school system and is safeguarded by the
awareness and concern of parents for their children's rights. Interaction of parents, teachers, and librarians provides a viable program for the education of disabled children. Administrators,
librarians, and teachers must combine their efforts to provide
necessary materials. Books in special formats are available from
many sources, but these materials are only effective when utilized
by the student and teacher. For many students books in special
formats have opened doors they thought closed because they did
not have access to the knowledge imparted by the printed word.
Talking books and reading machines are broadening the horizons
of many handicapped persons, but students must be educated as to
the availability and potentiality of these services and equipment in
order to utilize them to their fullest. Much of NLS's literature bears
the slogan "Reading is for Everyone." With the numerous materials
available there is no reason this cannot be true.

References

American Printing House for the Blind. *Central Catalog*. 11th ed. 2 vols.
    Louisville, Ky.: American Printing House for the Blind, 1980.
Hahn, Ellen Zabel. "Serving Blind and Physically Handicapped Readers: A
    Shared Responsibility. *Information Reports and Bibliographies* 7
    (February 1978): 41-42.
Kurzweil Computer Products. *Print to Speech*. Cambridge, Md.: Kurzweil
    Computer Products, 1979.

Library of Congress. Division for the Blind and Physically Handicapped. *Application for Free Library Service*. Washington, D.C.: Library of Congress, 1973.

National Braille Association. *Braille Book Bank Textbook Catalog, 1978-1979*. Rochester, N.Y.: National Braille Association, 1979.

National Library Service for the Blind and Physically Handicapped. "Facts." Washington, D.C.: Government Printing Office. Typewritten. January 1980.

_____. "A Scope of History." *Talking Book Topics*, May-June 1980, p. 3.

_____. *Library Resources for the Blind and Physically Handicapped*. Washington, D.C.: Library of Congress, 1979.

Recording for the Blind. *Information for New Borrowers*. New York: Recording for the Blind, 1979.

Telesensory Systems, Inc. *Optacon: A Reading System for the Blind*. Palo Alto: Telesensory Systems, Inc., 1979.

_____. "Speech +." Palo Alto: Telesensory Systems, Inc., 1976.

Velleman, Ruth A. *Serving Physically Disabled People: An Information Handbook for All Librarians*. New York: Bowker, 1979.

APPENDIX I.

SELECTED LIST OF GOALS AND ACTIVITIES FOR USE WITH HANDICAPPED STUDENTS

The Education of All Handicapped Children Act, Public Law 94-142, which became effective in 1978, mandates that handicapped children with exceptional educational needs be educated in the least restrictive environment. The enactment of this law has added new dimensions to the roles of school library media specialists. Media specialists now must work with special education teachers and regular classroom teachers to meet the individual needs of all children in the school.

Listed below are some goals and activities that have been used successfully to emphasize the unique abilities of handicapped students and provide optimum learning experiences for special children.

The activities for students are grouped under the developmental headings of socialization and behavior goals or academic skills. Each entry includes the objective, activities, and resources. Also listed are activities for parent involvement and a sample book talk activity, with a list of selected resources.

Socialization and Behavior Goals

I. *Objective*: To initiate and maintain effective peer group relationships such as taking turns and sharing.

   Activity: The concept of taking turns is introduced by playing a game of musical chairs with a small group of primary children including two behavioral disordered children who have been mainstreamed into the media center for one class period. After playing the game, a short discussion is held to answer questions such as: what happens when everyone tries to sit down?; what always happens when there is not enough of anything?; and why should we take turns? After the discussion the group is shown a filmstrip for reinforcement of concept.

On succeeding days the media specialist reads related storybooks such as *The Day I Had to Play with My Sister* by Crosby Bonsall or *If It Weren't for You* by Charlotte Zolotow.

II. *Objective*: To acquaint students with each other to encourage recognition of unique individual characteristics that are meaningful in developing a positive self-image.

Activity 1: Each student chooses one thing (job, sport, hobby, and so on) that he or she does well. In turn, each student is to pantomime that activity for the group. After each pantomime, the group will try to guess what the special thing is.

Activity 2: Each child is given a tree form cut out of green paper. The children look for pictures in old magazines that might represent (a) things that make them happy, (b) things that make them sad, (c) things they don't like, and so forth. The children decorate the tree with as many pictures as they wish which also tell about themselves.

Books to share related to this activity are *Hester the Jester* by Ben Sheeter and *The Me I See* by Barbara Hazen.

III. *Objective*: To develop self-confidence and a sense of self-worth.

Activity: Puppets with unique personality profiles are used to introduce children to differences among others. The media specialist creates dialogue using a different voice and personality to provide instruction and/or alleviate feelings of anxiety, frustration, or confusion on the part of the children. Especially helpful are the puppets from the kit, *On Stage: Wally, Bertha and You*. Wally is a green walrus and Bertha is a yellow ostrich. In addition to their odd colors, they have other physical and emotional problems which can be used as springboards for discussion and dramatics geared toward helping both handicapped and nonhandicapped children accept differences in others.

Academic Skills

I. *Objective*: To participate in group processes using body skills and symbolic representations of experiences and concepts.

Activity 1: Learning centers are set up in the media center with children given directions via cassette recordings. Activities at the center include arranging cartoon frames in sequential order, listening to a recorded story, and responding with appropriate answers to questions indicating satisfactory comprehension. For example, the media specialist begins to tell a story and the children contribute what comes next.

Activity 2: A child looks at a picture in which people are doing things backward and identifies what's wrong in the picture. A child draws a picture and deliberately leaves out an important item. The group tries to guess what is missing.

II.   *Objective*:   To participate with basic expression-language concepts.

Activity 1: Cassette recording of selected titles are provided for visually impaired students. After listening to the stories each student is given a blank cassette on which to record his or her responses to discussion questions asked by a peer tutor. The student is given the opportunity to record any other information about the story he or she wishes to share. Informal discussions between students who have listened to or read the same story are often taped and experience charts in large print are made.

Activity 2: A cadre of peer tutors is established in the media center to assist the handicapped student. The peer tutors are often paired with students of like interests, backgrounds, and so on. The handicapped student also serves in the peer tutoring program. For example, the older behavioral disordered student can read or tell stories to small groups of primary students.

The student serving as peer tutor is required to select and read a title from a prepared list. The media specialist suggests follow-up activities and assists in acquiring any materials needed. One such activity is the cooking of pancakes after sharing *Pancakes for Breakfast* by Tomie DePaola.

III.   *Objective*:   To participate in media center routines with functional concepts and body coordination.

Activity: Students view filmstrips and participate in hands-on experiences with audiovisual equipment. As mastery is achieved sessions are held during which the individual student demonstrates his or her skill in operating the equipment. The media specialist places a star or other symbol next to the name of each piece of equipment which the student can successfully operate. The student is then issued a laminated copy of the "license" authorizing his or her independent use of the equipment.

Parent Involvement

I. *Objective*:   To facilitate the development of positive parent attitudes
                    toward the school.

    Activity: Special invitations are sent to the parents of handicapped
    children to attend the school's annual book fair. At the book fair,
    parents are assisted in making selections of books for their special
    children. Book lists of titles for reading aloud are distributed and
    parents are allowed to check out books from the school media center.
    Parents also serve as volunteers to assist during the book fair, field
    trips, and for routine media center tasks.

    A pamphlet file is maintained so that information from national and
    local organizations offering help and service to handicapped people is
    readily available. A listing of the names and addresses of these or-
    ganizations is sent to parents for reference. Notices about resources
    within the community and how their children can make use of them are
    regularly sent to parents.

II. *Objective*:   To provide an opportunity for parents to acquire in-
                    expensive materials for home instruction use.

    Activity: Periodically parents are invited to participate in a parent
    game day. Special education and regular classroom teachers submit
    games or game ideas to be produced. The media center staff secures all
    materials needed and places materials, written instructions for how to
    make the games, and prototypes of the various games in the media
    preparation room. Parents are asked to assemble two of each game;
    one to leave in the media center, and one to carry home to use with
    their own child. Parents are allowed to make as many different games
    as they like or as their time schedule permits. Simple instructions for
    game use are supplied on three by five index cards.

Book Talks

I. *Objective*:   To help the nonhandicapped children understand and
                    accept the handicapping conditions of others.

    Activity: The media specialist will present book talks from one or more
    titles from a prepared bibliography of books about handicapped
    children. Prior to the scheduled book talk bulletin boards and/or
    displays are set up to allow children to voice concerns or ask questions
    about handicapping conditions.

    Older students are allowed to work in groups to review books
    assigned from the prepared bibliography. Each student reads the book

and writes a brief report. The group then discusses the different reports and compiles a group report including such things as feelings the book elicited, new facts learned, changes in opinions, and so on.

Selected Resources

Books for Media Specialists

Forte, Imogene. *Nooks, Crannies, and Corners*. Nashville: Incentive Publications, 1972.
_____. *Center Stuff from Nooks, Crannies, and Corners*. Nashville: Incentive Publications, 1973.
_____. *Kid's Stuff: Reading and Writing Readiness*. Nashville: Incentive Publications, 1975.
Platts, Mary E. *Spice*. Stevensville, Mich.: Educational Service, Inc., 1973.

Audiovisuals

Basic Library Skills: Audiovisuals. Boulder, Colo.: Learning Tree Filmstrips, 1978.
First Things . . . You Got Mad; Are You Glad? New York: Guidance Associates, 1970.
Mixing in (Kindle Four). Englewood Cliffs, N.J.: Scholastic/Kindle, 1974.
On Stage: Wally, Bertha, and You. Chicago: E. B. E. Corporation, 1971.

Books for Students

Bonsall, Crosby. *The Day I Had to Play with My Sister*. New York: Harper & Row, 1972.
Carle, Eric. *Pancakes, Pancakes*. New York: Pantheon, 1975.
DePaola, Tomie. *Pancakes for Breakfast*. New York: Harcourt Brace and Jovanovich, 1978.
_____. *The Popcorn Book*. New York: Holiday, 1978.
Hazen, Barbara Shook. *The Me I See*. Nashville: Abingdon Press, 1978.
Sheeter, Ben. *Hester the Jester*. New York: Harper & Row, 1977.
Zolotow, Charlotte. *If It Weren't For You*. New York: Harper & Row, 1966.

APPENDIX II.

DIRECTORY OF
SELECTED SOURCES
FOR MATERIALS

Alexander Graham Bell Association for the Deaf
3417 Volta Place, N.W.
Washington, DC 20007

American Printing House for the Blind, Inc.
1839 Frankfort Avenue
Louisville, KY 40206

Apollo Lasers
Electronic Visual Aids
6357 Arizona Circle
Los Angeles, CA 90045

Bell and Howell Company
Micro Photo Division
Old Mansfield Road
Wooster, OH 44691

Captioned Films for the Deaf Distribution Center
5034 Wisconsin Avenue, N.W.
Washington, DC 20016

Council for Exceptional Children
1920 Association Drive
Reston, VA 22091

Gallaudet College
Kendell Green
Washington, DC 20002

G. K. Hall and Company, Inc.
70 Lincoln Street
Boston, MA 02111

Handicapped Learner Materials Distribution Center (HLMDC)
Audio-Visual Center
Indiana University
Bloomington, IN 47405

Harper & Row Publishers
Department 61
10 East 53rd Street
New York, NY 10022

Joyce Motion Picture Company
8613 Yolanda Avenue
P.O. Box 458
Northridge, CA 91324

Keith Jennison Books/Franklin Watts, Inc.
845 Third Avenue
New York, NY 10022

Kurzweil Computers Products
Reading Machine Department
33 Cambridge Parkway
Cambridge, MA 02142

Library Reproduction Service
Microfilm Company of California
1977 South Los Angeles Street
Los Angeles, CA 90011

National Association for Mental Health
1800 North Kent Street
Rosslyn Station
Arlington, VA 22209

National Association of the Deaf
814 Thayer Avenue
Silver Spring, MD 20910

National Braille Association
Braille Book Bank
422 Clinton Avenue, South
Rochester, NY 14620

National Braille Association
Braille Technical Tables Bank
31610 Evergreen Road
Birmingham, MI 48009

National Center for Law and the Handicapped
211 West Washington Street
South Bend, IN 46601

National Clearinghouse for Mental Health Information
National Institute of Mental Health
5600 Fishers Lane
Rockville, MD 20850

National Federation of the Blind
218 Randolph Hotel Building
Des Moines, IA 50309

National Information Center for Special Education Materials (NICSEM)
University of Southern California
University Park
Los Angeles, CA 90007

National Library Services for the Blind and Physically Handicapped
Library of Congress
1291 Taylor Street, N.W.
Washington, DC 20542

Office of Handicapped Individuals
Department of Health, Education, and Welfare
Washington, DC 20201

Recordings for the Blind
215 East 58th Street
New York, NY 10022

R. R. Bowker and Company
1180 Avenue of the Americas
New York, NY 10036

Telesensory Systems, Inc.
1889 Page Mill Road
Palo Alto, CA 94304

Ulverscroft Large Print Books
Oscar B. Stiskin, U.S. Agent
P.O. Box 3055
Stamford, CT 06905

Volunteer Services for the Blind
919 Walnut Street
Philadelphia, PA 19107

Volunteer Transcribing Service
205 East Third Avenue, Suite 201
San Mateo, CA 94401

APPENDIX III.

SELECTED LIST
OF ORGANIZATIONS

Alexander Graham Bell Association for the Deaf
3417 Volta Place, N.W.
Washington, DC 20007

American Association for Health, Physical Education and Recreation
    Programs for the Handicapped
Information and Research Utilization Center
1201 Sixteenth Street, N.W.
Washington, DC 20036

American Association for the Education of the Severely/Profoundly
    Handicapped
P.O. Box 15287
Seattle, WA 98115

American Foundation for the Blind, Inc.
15 West 16th Street
New York, NY 10011

American Speech and Hearing Association
9030 Old Georgetown Road
Washington, DC 20014

Association for Children with Learning Disabilities (ACLD)
5224 Grace Street
Pittsburg, PA 15236

Boy Scouts of America
Scouting for the Handicapped Division
North Brunswick, NH 08902

Braille Institute of America, Inc.
741 North Vermont Avenue
Los Angeles, CA 90029

Bureau of Education for the Handicapped
Office of Education
Department of Health, Education, and Welfare
Washington, DC 20202

Children's Defense Fund
1763 R Street, N.W.
Washington, DC 20009

Council for Exceptional Children
1920 Association Drive
Reston, VA 22091

Friends of Handicapped Children
3877 Shasta Street
P.O. Drawer 99490
San Diego, CA 92102

Girl Scouts of the U.S.A.
Scouting for Handicapped Girls Program
830 Third Avenue
New York, NY 10022

Joseph P. Kennedy, Jr. Foundation
1701 K Street, N.W., Suite 205
Washington, DC 20006

Mainstream, Inc.
1200 15th Street, N.W.
Washington, DC 20005

Mental Health Association (MHA)
1800 North Kent Street
Arlington, VA 22209

National Center for a Barrier-Free Environment
8401 Connecticut Avenue, Suite 402
Washington, DC 20015

National Association for Hearing and Speech Action (NAHSA)
6110 Executive Boulevard
Rockville, MD 20852

National Association for Retarded Children
420 Lexington Avenue
New York, NY 10017

National Association for Visually Handicapped (NAVH)
305 East 24th Street, 17-C
New York, NY 10010

National Association of the Deaf (NAD)
814 Thayer Avenue
Silver Spring, MD 20910

National Center for Law and the Handicapped
211 West Washington Street
South Bend, IN 46601

National Easter Seal Society for Crippled Children and Adults
2023 West Ogden Avenue
Chicago, IL 60612

National Federation of the Blind (NFB)
218 Randolph Hotel Building
Des Moines, IA 50309

National Information Center for the Handicapped
P.O. Box 1492
Washington, DC 20013

National Library Service for the Blind and Physically Handicapped
Library of Congress
1291 Taylor Street, N.W.
Washington, DC 20542

The National Media Materials Center for Severely Handicapped Persons
P.O. Box 318
George Peabody College
Nashville, TN 37203

Speech Foundation of America
152 Lombardy Road
Memphis, TN 38111

Telephone Pioneers of America
83 Maiden Lane
New York, NY 10038

U.S. Architectural and Transportation Barrier Compliance Board
330 Connecticut Avenue, S.W.
Washington, DC 20201

APPENDIX IV.

THE FOUNDATION CENTER: NATIONAL AND COOPERATING COLLECTIONS

The Foundation Center operates a library in New York and Washington, D.C., which contains the public records and printed publications related to private foundations. There are cooperating collections, which are open to the public, in all fifty states.

National Collections

The Foundation Center
888 Seventh Avenue
New York, NY 10019

The Foundation Center
1001 Connecticut Avenue, N.W.
Washington, DC 20036

Cooperating Collections

Alabama

Birmingham Public Library
2020 Seventh Avenue, North
Birmingham, AL 35023

Arkansas

Little Rock Public Library
Reference Department
700 Louisiana Street
Little Rock, AR 72201

California

San Diego Public Library
820 E. Street
San Diego, CA 92101

San Francisco Public Library
Business Branch
530 Kearney Street
San Francisco, CA 94108
(Also covers Alaska, Arizona, Colorado, Hawaii, Idaho, Montana,
Nevada, Oregon, Utah, and Washington.)

University Research Library
Reference Department
University of California
Los Angeles, CA 90024

Colorado

Denver Public Library
Sociology Division
1357 Broadway
Denver, CO 80203

Connecticut

Hartford Public Library
Reference Department
500 Main Street
Hartford, CT 06103

Florida

Jacksonville Public Library
Business, Science, and Industry Department
122 North Ocean Street
Jacksonville, FL 32202

Miami-Dade Public Library, Florida Collection
One Biscayne Boulevard
Miami, FL 33132

Georgia

Atlanta Public Library
126 Carnegie Way, N.W.
Atlanta, GA 30303
(Also covers Alabama, Florida, South Carolina, and Tennessee.)

Hawaii

Thomas Hale Hamilton Library
Humanities and Social Sciences Division
2550 The Mall
Honolulu, HI 96822

Idaho

Caldwell Public Library
1010 Dearborn Street
Caldwell, ID 83605

Illinois

Sangamon State University Library
Shepherd Road
Springfield, IL 62708

Indiana

Indianapolis-Marion County Public Library
40 East St. Clair Street
Indianapolis, IN 46204

Iowa

Des Moines Public Library
100 Locust Street
Des Moines, IA 50309

Kansas

Topeka Public Library
Adult Services Department
1515 West 10th Street
Topeka, KS 66604

Kentucky

Louisville Free Public Library
Fourth and York Streets
Louisville, KY 40203

Louisiana

New Orleans Public Library
Business and Science Division
219 Loyola Avenue
New Orleans, LA 70140

Maine

University of Maine at Portland-Gorham
Center for Research and Advance Study
246 Deering Avenue
Portland, ME 04102

Maryland

Enoch Pratt Free Library
Social Science and History Department
Baltimore, MD 21201

Massachusetts

Associated Foundation of Greater Boston
204 Washington Street, Suite 501
Boston, MA 02108

Boston Public Library
Copley Square
Boston, MA 02117

Michigan

Henry Ford Centennial Library
15301 Michigan Avenue
Dearborn, MI 48126

Grand Rapids Public Library
Sociology and Education Department
Library Plaza
Grand Rapids, MI 49502

Purdy Library
Wayne State University
Detroit, MI 48202

Minnesota

Minneapolis Public Library
Sociology Department
300 Nicollet Mall
Minneapolis, MN 55401
(Also covers North and South Dakota.)

Mississippi

Jackson Metropolitan Library
301 North State Street
Jackson, MS 39201

Missouri

The Danforth Foundation Library
222 South Central Avenue
St. Louis, MO 63105

Kansas City Public Library
311 East 12th Street
Kansas City, MO 64106
(Also covers Kansas.)

Montana

Eastern Montana College Library
Reference Department
Billings, MT 59101

Nebraska

W. Dale Clark Library
Social Sciences Department
215 South 15th Street
Omaha, NE 68102

New Hampshire

The New Hampshire Charitable Fund
One South Street
Concord, NH 03301

New Jersey

New Jersey State Library
Reference Section
185 West State Street
Trenton, NJ 08625

New Mexico

New Mexico State Library
300 Don Gaspar Street
Santa Fe, NM 87501

New York

Buffalo and Erie County Public Library
Lafayette Square
Buffalo, NY 14203

Levittown Public Library
Reference Department
One Bluegrass Lane
Levittown, NY 11657

New York State Library
State Education Department
Education Building
Albany, NY 12224

Rochester Public Library
Business and Social Science Division
115 South Avenue
Rochester, NY 14604

North Carolina

William R. Perkins Library
Duke University
Durham, NC 27706

Ohio

The Cleveland Foundation Library
700 National City Bank Building
Cleveland, OH 44114

Oklahoma

Oklahoma City Community Foundation
1300 North Broadway
Oklahoma City, OK 73103

Tulsa City-County Library System
400 Civic Center
Tulsa, OK 74103

Oregon

Library Association of Portland
Education and Psychology Department
801 S.W. 10th Avenue
Portland, OR 97205

Pennsylvania

The Free Library of Philadelphia
Logan Square
Philadelphia, PA 19103
(Also covers Delaware.)

Hillman Library
University of Pittsburgh
Pittsburgh, PA 15213

Rhode Island

Providence Public Library
Reference Department
150 Empire Street
Providence, RI 02903

South Carolina

South Carolina State Library
Reader Services Department
1500 Senate Street
Columbia, SC 29211

Tennessee

Memphis Public Library
1850 Peabody Avenue
Memphis, TN 38104

Texas

Dallas Public Library
History and Social Sciences Division
1954 Commerce Street
Dallas, TX 75201
(Also covers Arkansas, Louisiana, New Mexico, and Oklahoma.)

The Hogg Foundation for Mental Health
University of Texas
Austin, TX 78712

Minnie Stevens Piper Foundation
201 North St. Mary's Street
San Antonio, TX 78205

Utah

Salt Lake City Public Library
Information and Adult Services
209 East 5th Street
Salt Lake City, UT 84111

Vermont

State of Vermont Department of Libraries
Reference Services Unit
111 State Street
Montpelier, VT 05602

Virginia

Richmond Public Library
Business, Science, & Technology Department
101 East Franklin Street
Richmond, VA 23219

Washington

Seattle Public Library
1000 4th Avenue
Seattle, WA 98104

West Virginia

Kanawha County Public Library
123 Capitol Street
Charleston, WV 25301

Wisconsin

   Marquette University Memorial Library
   1415 West Wisconsin Avenue
   Milwaukee, WI 53233
   (Also covers Illinois.)

Wyoming

   Laramie County Community College Library
   1400 East College Drive
   Cheyenne, WY 82001

Puerto Rico

   Consumer Education and Service Center
   Department of Consumer Affairs
   Minillas Central Government Building North
   Santurce, PR 00918
   (Covers selected foundations.)

Mexico

   Biblioteca Benjamin Franklin
   Londres 16
   Mexico 6, D.F.
   Mexico
   (Covers selected foundations.)

SELECTED ANNOTATED BIBLIOGRAPHY

The Blind

Bartholemew, Cecilia. *Second Sight*. New York: Putnam's, 1980. (Young Adult.) Roz Tinde, a successful fashion model at twenty-six, discovers that she has a degenerative eye disease. She buys a three-apartment house in a poor neighborhood and works with carpenters to make it a safe, comfortable home for a blind person. But Roz soon gets silent messages on her phone, followed by messages that she doesn't belong in the neighborhood. Her old boyfriend wants her dead because he has been playing investment games with her money. He is arrested in the end and Roz is safe.

Brown, Marion Marsh, and Corne, Ruth. *The Silent Storm*. Nashville: Abingdon Press, 1963. (Intermediate.) This lightly fictionalized biography of Anne Sullivan presents a good picture of the treatment received by the physically handicapped (blind and deaf) around the turn of the century.

Butler, Beverly Kathleen. *Gift of Gold*. New York: Dodd, Mead, 1972. (Intermediate.) Cathy Wheeler is studying to be a physical therapist but her blindness causes many obstacles.

_____. *Light a Single Candle*. New York: Dodd, Mead, 1962. (Intermediate.) The difficulties of accepting blindness, training a guide dog, and moving through a sighted world are described with insight and sympathy. The story is about a fourteen-year-old girl.

Christopher, Matt. *Stranded*. Boston: Little, Brown & Co., 1974. (Elementary.) After his family's boat is wrecked in a storm, Andy, who is blind, manages to survive on a tropical island until he is rescued.

Cleaver, Vera, and Cleaver, Bill. *Mimosa Tree*. Philadelphia: Lippincott, 1970. (Intermediate.) Because her father is blind, fourteen-year-old Marvella is forced to become head of the family when her stepmother abandons them.

Concoran, Barbara. *The Long Journey*. Illus. by Charles Robinson. New New York: Atheneum, 1970. (Elementary-Intermediate.) Laurie's grandfather finally acknowledges concern about his rapidly diminishing vision. He sends Laurie across Montana on a horse to find her uncle, who is her only other relative. Laurie has several adventures along the way. When she finds her uncle, he has remarried and wants to adopt her. Her grandfather eventually consents to cataract surgery and the family plans a permanent reunion.

Dickinson, Peter. *Annerton Pit*. Boston: Little, Brown & Co., 1977. (Young Adult and Adult.) An adventurous story line which leads Jake, who is blind, to an abandoned mine. Jake has special means of adapting to his limitations and cultivating his abilities.

Gill, Derek. *Tom Sullivan's Adventures in Darkness*. New York: New American Library, 1977. (Intermediate.) Tom accepts his blindness as a challenge, not a setback.

Heide, Florence. *Sound of Sunshine, Sound of Rain*. New York: Four Winds, 1970. (Preschool and Primary.) A blind boy finds life a joy. This sensitive story is very effective if read aloud.

Hunter, Edith Fisher. *Child of the Silent Night*. Boston: Houghton Mifflin Co., 1963. (Intermediate.) This short, easy-to-read biography demonstrates that a person can learn and achieve despite handicaps such as blindness and deafness. The education of Laura Bridgman was the first breakthrough in the instruction of a blind, deaf, mute person.

Jenson, Virginia Allen and Haller, Dorcas Woodbury. *What's That?* New York: Philomel, 1979. (Preschool and Primary.) Children who are visually impaired or blind have an opportunity to touch the characters Little Rough, Little Spot, and their friends.

Keats, Ezra Jack. *Apt. 3* New York: Macmillan, 1971. (Elementary.) Two young brothers hear music and decide to see if they can find where it comes from. They trace the sound to the apartment of a blind man who is playing the harmonica. The children are astonished at what the blind man can learn about the world through his hearing and what he can say about it through his music.

Litchfield, Ada B. *A Cane in Her Hand*. Chicago: Whitman, 1977. (Preschool and Primary.) A visually impaired child learns to use a cane
and improve her mobility in spite of difficulties in accepting it and
experiencing adult insensitivity.

MacLachlan, Patricia. *Through Grandpa's Eyes*. New York: Harper &
Row, 1980. (Elementary.) The relationship between John and his
blind grandfather is special. The story tells of John's life with his
grandfather.

Mathis, Sharon Bell. *Listen for the Fig Tree*. New York: Viking Press, 1970.
(Young Adult.) A sensitive narrative about the world of a blind girl
and her friend.

Miklish, Rita. *Sugar Bee*. New York: Delacorte Press, 1972. (Elementary.)
Sugar Bee cannot accept Rosemary's ability to see beauty despite her
blindness.

Milton, Hilary. *Blind Flight*. New York: Franklin Watts, 1980. (Intermediate.) Thirteen-year-old Debbie is faced with landing her pilot
uncle's small plane after he is knocked unconscious by a bird that
crashed through the windshield. Debbie has never flown a plane by
herself and is blinded by cataracts. Through a radio she manages to
get help. Readers are drawn into the anxiety of those on the ground
as they work to land the plane and its two passengers safely.

Paton Walsh, Jill. *Goldengrove*. New York: Farrar, Straus and Giroux,
1972. (Young Adult.) Madge and Paul spend the summer at their
grandparents' home near the sea. They meet Ralph, a blind professor, who is trying to finish a manuscript. Madge is drawn to him
and decides to stay with him.

Peterson, Pale. *Sally Can't See*. New York: John Day, 1977. (Preschool
and Primary.) A twelve-year-old blind girl learns to read, swim, and
ride a horse.

Thomas, William E. *The New Boy Is Blind*. New York: Messner, 1980.
(Elementary.) Mrs. Conboy reluctantly leaves her blind son in his
new class with sighted children. She overprotects him, making new
adjustments difficult for Rickey, but finally she allows Rickey's
fuller participation in school events. The problems of a child
adjusting to a mainstreamed class are handled skillfully here.

Vinson, Kathryn. *Run with the Ring*. New York: Harcourt, Brace, 1965.
(Intermediate.) The boy in this book is interested in sports and
electronics and believes both areas are closed to him when he
becomes blind. He is skeptical and bitter until he learns that he can
make a new life for himself—one not too different from the life he
was planning.

Wolf, Bernard. *Connie's New Eyes*. Philadelphia: J. B. Lippincott, 1976. (Intermediate.) The author follows Blythe, a golden retriever, from puppyhood, through her training as a seeing-eye dog, to her new life with her blind mistress, Connie.

Wosmek, Frances. *A Bowl of Sun*. Chicago: Children's Press, 1976. (Elementary.) Being blind had never troubled Megan until her safe world was disrupted by a move to the city and starting school.

The Deaf

Arthur, Catherine. *My Sister's Silent World*. Chicago: Children's Press, 1979. (Middle or Intermediate.) A big sister's description of her sister's hearing problem.

Coolidge, Olivia Enson. *Come by Here*. Boston: Houghton Mifflin Co., 1970. (Intermediate.) Six-year-old Minty Payson is deaf. The suppression of her emotions and the immediate punishment for any open expression of these emotions builds in Minty a hatred and distrust of all people. The reader is immediately drawn to sympathize with Minty's plight. The desire to help Minty and the frustration of not being able to do so may cause intense reader reaction to this thought-provoking drama.

Corcoran, Barbara. *A Dance to Still Music*. New York: Atheneum, 1974. (Intermediate.) Sudden complete deafness causes Margaret to run away, but a wounded deer and an old woman help her return to the world of sound.

Goldfeder, Cheryl and Goldfeder, James. *The Girl Who Wouldn't Talk*. Silver Spring, Md.: National Association of the Deaf, 1974. (Preschool and Primary.) Robin, a deaf girl, is unhappy when she is sent to a school for the deaf but learns sign language and is no longer sad.

Hanlon, Emily. *The Swing*. Scarsdale, N.Y.: Bradbury, 1979. (Young Adult and Adult.) An eleven-year-old deaf girl and a thirteen-year-old boy with family problems seek refuge at a swing which has come to have a special meaning for each of them.

Harris, Rosemary. *The Bright and Morning Star*. New York: Macmillan, 1972. (Young Adult.) In ancient Egypt a young boy, Sadhi, becomes deaf and mute after a sickness. Sadhi's mother takes him to the king's healer, Hekhti. Hekhti finds out a plot against the king and uses Sadhi to rescue him.

Levine, Betty. *A Griffon's Nest*. New York: Macmillan, 1975. (Young Adult.) Two children travel back through time to the seventh century where they encounter Nessa, a deaf girl, who leads them through a series of harrowing adventures.

Levine, Edna S. *Lisa and Her Soundless World*. New York: Human Science, 1974. (Young Adult.) Lisa is a little girl with impaired hearing who learns to use and understand speech.

MacIntrye, Elizabeth. *The Purple Mouse*. New York: Elsevier-Nelson, 1975. (Elementary.) Because of a hearing loss, Hattie was shy until she met a spunky, purple mouse who was different from his peers too.

Montgomery, Elizabeth Rider. *The Mystery of the Boy Next Door*. New Canaan, CT: Garrard, 1978. (Intermediate.) This book presents a serious disability in a sensitive and interesting manner. A chart of the deaf hand-symbol alphabet included at the back of the book adds interest.

Peter, Diana. *Claire and Emma*. New York: John Day, 1977. (Preschool and Primary.) Two deaf sisters learn to lip-read and speak.

Peterson, Jeanne Whitehouse. *I Have a Sister, My Sister Is Deaf*. New York: Harper & Row, 1977. (Preschool and Primary.) A young girl talks in a gentle but realistic way about her little sister who is deaf, and what she can and cannot do.

Robinson, Veronica. *David in Silence*. Philadelphia: Lippincott, 1965. (Young Adult.) Eric and his younger brother David, who is deaf, move to Birmingham, England. David makes friends with Michael, who tries to communicate with David through finger spelling and mime. David runs into a dark tunnel and gets lost, but Michael finds him. Later, David ventures back into the tunnel to prove there was nothing to be afraid of and this causes his status with his group of friends to improve.

Sesame Street Sign Language Fun. New York: Random House, 1980. (Preschool and Primary.) Muppet illustrations are accompanied by Linda Bove signing the words and phrases. The text groups words into concept groups like color, opposites, school, family, and so on. This book is useful to reinforce word-picture association with both hearing and deaf children. Endpapers carry the finger spelling alphabet and numbers from one to ten.

Spence, Eleanor. *The Nothing Place*. New York: Harper & Row, 1973. (Intermediate.) When Glen suffers a hearing loss following an illness, his friends raise money to buy him a hearing aid.

Wolf, Bernard. *Anna's Silent World*. Philadelphia: Lippincott, 1977. (Preschool and Primary.) Anna, who is deaf, learns to function normally with the assistance of people and machines.

The Mentally Handicapped

Albert, Louise. *But I'm Ready to Go*. New York: Dell, 1978. (Intermediate.) Judy finds it difficult to understand her brain damage and the problems she will have finding her place in society.

Baldwin, Anne Norris. *A Little Time*. New York: Viking Press, 1978. (Young Adult and Adult.) Mattie, a four-year-old boy who has Down's Syndrome, is sent to a foster home for a stay. His family has a chance to reassess their feelings while he is away.

Branscum, Robbie. *For Love of Jody*. New York: Lothrop, Lee and Sheppard, 1979. (Intermediate.) Twelve-year-old Frankie overcomes her bitterness toward her mother and jealousy over her younger, mentally retarded sister.

Brightman, Alan. *Like Me*. Boston: Little, Brown & Co., 1976. (Preschool and Primary.) Color photo story of a retarded child who is aware that he learns slower than other children but wants very much to be accepted.

Brown, Roy. *Escape the River*. New York: Seaburg, 1972. (Also published as *The River*.) (Young Adult.) After Kenny was born retarded, his parents adopted Paul. The boys are left unsupervised most of the time and Paul assumes responsibility for Kenny. Feeling unwanted, the boys plan to run away, but when their plans fail they learn of their father's love for them.

Byars, Betsy. *Summer of the Swans*. New York: Viking Press, 1970. (Intermediate and Young Adult.) When Sara's mentally handicapped brother is lost, she realizes how petty her own personal troubles have been.

Carpelan, Bo Gustaf Bertelsson. *Bow Island: The Story of a Summer that Was Different*. New York: Delacorte Press, 1971. (Young Adult.) The first person narrative portrays a boy's friendship with a young man who is mentally retarded. The friendship is a satisfying one in which both young men grow in some way—Johan learning tolerance and Marvin learning to conquer fear.

———. *Dolphins in the City*. New York: Delacorte Press, 1976. (Young Adult and Adult.) A Finnish boy leaves an island and moves to the city. His friend, Johan, who is mentally retarded, must learn to cope with the greater demands of the city.

Cleaver, Vera, and Cleaver, Bill. *Me Too*. New York: New American Library, 1975. (Intermediate.) In one painful summer Lydia learns to accept her twin sister's mental handicap and father's desertion.

Dixon, Paige. *The Search for Charlie*. New York: Atheneum, 1976. (Intermediate.) Jane and her friend Vic search the Montana Rocky Mountains for her kidnapped brother, Charlie.

Fassler, Joan. *One Little Girl*. New York: Behavioral Publications, 1969. (Elementary.) Laurie is a "slow child" and this makes her feel unhappy. Her mother takes her to a doctor who reports that Laurie has difficulty with some tasks, but is adept at others. Soon Laurie notices adults are paying more attention to what she does well. This helps Laurie feel pride in herself.

Garrigue, Sheila. *Between Friends*. Scarsdale, N.Y.: Bradbury, 1978. (Intermediate.) A sensitive book providing insight into the ways people react to retarded persons, and a very special friendship between a retarded girl and a newly found friend.

Hamilton, Virginia. *The Planet of Junior Brown*. New York: Macmillan, 1971. (Intermediate.) Junior Brown is a very fat, very disturbed young black. He has one friend who is also a friend to many young black boys who live in abandoned houses all over the city. Junior's whole life is a nightmare and at the end of the story he is totally insane. Strange, complicated story of people who have been defeated by the world and who create their own planet in order to escape.

Henroid, Lorraine. *Special Olympics and Parolympics*. New York: Franklin Watts, 1979. (Intermediate.) This valuable book presents the special olympics for the mentally retarded and the parolympics for the physically handicapped.

Hersch, Karen. *My Sister*. Minneapolis: Carolrhoda Books, 1977. (Preschool and Primary.) A book to help children understand the mentally retarded and their siblings through a boy who is sometimes jealous of all the attention his deaf older sister receives.

Klein, Gerda. *The Blue Rose*. New York: Lawrence Hill, 1974. (Elementary.) Retarded Jenny is much loved by her family, but has trouble with her peers because her behavior seems inappropriate to them. Although her parents are concerned about her future they still enjoy the present happiness she brings them.

Lasker, Jor. *He's My Brother*. Chicago: Albert Whitman and Company, 1974. (Elementary.) A boy has a slow-learning younger brother, Jamie, who gets teased. Becka, the older sister, bakes brownies for him and is kind. The brother sometimes is impatient with Jamie, but then plays with him to make up for it. Jamie is good with babies and animals. The family is very good, loving, and patient with him.

Larsen, Hanne. *Don't Forget Tom*. New York: Thomas Y. Crowell & Co., 1978. (Elementary.) Straightforward text and photos explain Tom's mental handicap.

Little, Jean. *Take Wing*. Boston: Little, Brown & Co., 1968. (Intermediate and Young Adult.) This book describes the ambivalent feelings of

love and resentment that can exist between siblings, as well as the
oveprotectiveness of a mother who cannot accept her child's
handicap. This could help adults as well as children recognize,
understand, and deal with children who are retarded or "different"
in some way.

McCracken, Mary. *Lovey: A Very Special Child*. Philadelphia: J. B.
Lippincott, 1976. (Young Adult.) A true story of eight-year-old
Hannah's struggle toward a normal life in spite of being emotionally
disturbed.

Olminsky, Elaine. *Jon O: A Special Boy*. Englewood Cliffs, N.J.: Prentice-
Hall, 1977. (Preschool and Primary.) Jon O, an active eight-year-old
Down's Syndrome boy, is shown functioning in school and as a
family member with his two brothers with whom he has a good
relationship.

Posner, Grace. *In My Sister's Eyes*. New York: Beaufort Books, 1980.
(Young Adult.) Billy has a retarded epileptic sister who will soon be
temporarily staying at home. The story is of Billy, his friends, his
sister, and their problems.

Rinaldo, C. L. *Dark Dreams*. New York: Harper & Row, 1974. (Intermediate.) This touching story realistically portrays the prejudice
people may harbor toward the mentally handicapped. A child's fear
of a vicious bully and the numbing effect the dread produces are
described vividly as is the ability to overcome this fear.

Rodowki, Colby F. *What About Me?* New York: Franklin Watts, 1976.
(Young Adult.) Torn between love for her mongoloid brother and
feelings that she is neglected, confined, and ignored because of him,
Dorrie struggles through her sophomore year in high school.

Shyer, Marlene Fanta. *Welcome Home, Jellybean*. New York: Charles
Scribner's Sons, 1978. (Young Adult and Adult.) Thirteen-year-old
Gerri comes home to stay after spending her life in institutions. Her
younger brother narrates the story of what happens.

Smith, Gene. *The Hayburners*. New York: Delacorte Press, 1974. (Young
Adult.) Will gains compassion for the handicapped when Joey, a
retarded farm hand, helps him raise his runt steer.

Sobol, Harriet Langoam. *My Brother Steven Is Retarded*. New York:
Macmillan, 1977. (Preschool and Primary.) An honest book about a
retarded child and the love, anger, and concern that his sister feels
toward him.

Walker, Pamela. *Twyla*. Englewood Cliffs, N.J.: Prentice-Hall, 1973.
(Young Adult.) The death in an auto accident of Twyla Krotz, a
15-year-old retarded girl, is reported in the local newspaper.

Through her letters to Wally, a former student at the high school with whom she was infatuated, the events of her life are revealed.

Wrightson, Patricia. *A Racehorse for Andy*. New York: Harcourt, Brace, 1968. (Intermédiate.) Andy is a charming retarded boy who has grown up with no father and little parental guidance. Though he is marked as "different," he is still able to lead a fulfilling, happy life.

The Physically Handicapped

Adams, Barbara. *Like It Is*. New York: Walker & Co., 1979. (Young Adult.) A group of handicapped youngsters discuss their disabilities and how they cope with them.

Berger, Gilda. *Physical Disabilities*. New York: Franklin Watts, 1979. (Young Adult.) This book discusses a variety of physical disabilities, societal attitudes toward them, and legislation dealing with the problems of the disabled.

Blume, Judy. *Deenie*. Scarscale, N.Y.: Bradbury, 1973. (Young Adult.) Deenie, who has always been repelled by people with handicaps or deformities, discovers that she is suffering from sclerosis and will have to wear a spinal brace.

Brown, Fern G. *You're Somebody Special on a Horse*. Chicago: Whitman, 1977. (Intermediate.) Marni lives only for horses. Faced with losing her horse if her schoolwork does not improve, she has the chance to participate in a program that allows handicapped girls and boys the experience and thrill of riding.

Butler, Hal. *Sports Heroes Who Wouldn't Quit*. New York: Messner, 1973. (Intermediate.) Stories of fifteen athletes who overcame mental anguish or physical disabilities to become sports heroes.

Cavanna, Betty. *Joyride*. New York: William Morrow and Co., 1974. (Young Adult.) Susan was left lame by polio. Her high school friends, now greatly preoccupied with boys, see her as asocial and involve her less and less in their activities.

Cook, Marjorie. *To Walk on Two Feet*. Philadelphia: Westminster Press, 1978. (Middle or Intermediate.) After a car accident, Carrie has both legs amputated and must reenter high school and adjust to her disability.

Cragg, Sheila. *Run, Patty, Run*. New York: Harper & Row, 1980. (Young Adult.) Patty's father is determined no one calls her "handicapped" because of her epilepsy, so he pushes her to excel in long distance running. Avid runners may be interested in Patty's experiences, and handicapped young adults will be inspired by her story.

Fanshawe, Elizabeth. *Rachel*. Scarsdale, N.Y.: Bradbury, 1977. (Preschool and Primary.) Rachel must use a wheelchair but participates fully in school, ignoring the inconvenience.

Fassler, Joan. *Howie Helps Himself*. Chicago: Whitman, 1975. (Preschool and Primary.) Howie, who has cerebral palsy, wants to be able to move his wheelchair by himself.

Green, Phyllis. *Walkie Walkie*. Reading, Maine: Addison-Wesley, 1978. (Intermediate.) A story of two boys, each with their own severe but different handicap. One has cerebral palsy and the other is an emotionally troubled fourteen-year-old.

Hale, Glorya. *The Source Book for the Disabled*. New York: Paddington Press, 1979. (Young Adult.) An illustrated guide to easier and more independent living for the physically disabled, their family, and friends.

Harnishfeger, Lloyd. *Prisoner of the Mound Builders*. Minneapolis: Lerner Publications, 1973. (Young Adult.) A disabled hero has only one leg, which causes him difficulty in being an effective hunter.

Haskins, James. *The Quiet Revolution*. New York: Thomas Y. Crowell & Co., 1979. (Intermediate and Young Adult.) A history of the disabled movement from the early fifties to the present.

Jones, Ron. *The Acorn People*. New York: Bantam, 1977. (Young Adult and Adult.) Based on a true story, this inspirational book delightfully shows how five handicapped campers have a chance to show how strong and capable they are.

Kamien, Janet. *What if You Couldn't . . . ?* New York: Charles Scribner's Sons, 1979. (Intermediate.) This book about disabilities asks the reader to imagine that he or she is the disabled person and then introduces experiments that help to understand how it feels to have a disability. Hearing and visual impairments, physical handicaps, and emotional disturbances are among those included.

Lasker, Joe. *Nick Joins In*. Chicago: Whitman, 1980. (Preschool and Primary.) Confined to a wheelchair, Nick is going to public school for the first time. Not until he is involved in school activities and accepted by the other children does he feel comfortable. Nick is an independent little boy who does as much as he can do and doesn't worry excessively about what he can't do.

Lawrence, Mildred. *Touchmark*. New York: Harcourt, Brace, 1975. (Intermediate.) Abigail designs a homemade wheelchair for her friend Emily, enabling the girls to play a part in the Revolution.

Lee, Mildred. *The People Therein*. Boston: Houghton Mifflin Co., 1980. (Young Adult.) In 1910, eighteen-year-old Ailanthus lives in the

Great Smoky Mountains in her family's small cabin. She's a thoughtful girl who keeps to herself because she is lame. She is chastised when she refuses the marriage proposal of a boy she doesn't love. She soon falls in love with a teacher, Drew. Drew has to leave the mountains to go to Boston to take care of a dying relative, but returns after a while to Ailanthus.

Matthew, Christopher. *The Long-Haired Boy*. New York: Atheneum, 1980. (Young Adult.) Hugh Fleming is the "Long-Haired Boy," a term used for the university-educated men who were to become Britain's fighter pilots. He commits a foolish mistake and is shot down. He survives the crash to discover that he has been horribly disfigured and has lost the use of his hands. Hugh's rehabilitation is a learning process in which his greatest battle is against self-pity.

Phelan, Terry Wolfe. *The S. S. Vallentine*. Englewood Cliffs, N.J.: Four Winds Press, 1979. (Intermediate.) Connie, who is in a wheelchair, comes to class and the students don't know how to act toward her.

Phipson, Joan. *A Tide Flowing*. New York: Atheneum, 1981. (Young Adult.) After Mark's mother dies, he goes to live with his grandparents and becomes friends with Connie, a young quadriplegic. With Connie he can share the world that interests him, the world of nature.

Richard, Adrienne. *Wings*. Boston: Little, Brown & Co., 1974. (Young Adult.) Harold is missing two fingers; his teacher responds with excessive protectiveness.

Savitz, Harriet M. *On the Move*. New York: Aron, 1979. (Young Adult.) Since her recovery from polio, Carrie Dennis has been confined to a wheelchair. She rarely leaves her house and her social contacts are restricted to her family.

Slepian, Jan. *The Alfred Summer*. New York: Macmillan, 1980. (Young Adult.) Their homemade boat won't float, dashing a getaway dream, but a burdened boy and his handicapped helpers learn to launch themselves one unforgettable Coney Island summer.

Smith, Doris Buchanan. *Kelly's Creek*. New York: Thomas Y. Crowell & Co., 1975. (Intermediate.) Kelly has a learning disability that makes it difficult for him to coordinate hands, eyes, feet, and speech. But he is able to overcome some of his problems in a very simple way.

Sullivan, M. B. *Feeling Free*. Reading, Maine: Addison-Wesley, 1979. (Intermediate.) This book features essays by five children with various handicaps—blindness, deafness, dyslexia, cerebral palsy, and dwarfism.

Wartski, Maureen Crane. *My Brother Is Special*. Philadelphia: West-minster Press, 1979. (Intermediate.) A story of how the disability of one family member impinges on other family members, especially the siblings.

White, Paul. *Janet at School*. New York: Thomas Y. Crowell & Co., 1978. (Preschool and Primary.) Five-year-old Janet is successfully main-streamed into a regular classroom with the support of family, friends, and her teacher, although she has spina bifida (open spinal cord).

Witter, Evelyn. *Claw Foot*. Minneapolis: Lerner Publications, 1976. (Intermediate.) Claw Foot, a crippled Sioux chieftain's son, sets out to save his people from starvation and gain a name of respect.

INDEX

PUBLICATIONS
OF THE
CONTRIBUTORS

Barbara Baskin

Baskin, Barbara, and Harris, Karen. *The Special Child in the Library*. Chicago: American Library Association, 1976.

_____. *Notes From a Different Drummer: A Guide to Juvenile Fiction Portraying the Handicapped*. New York: Bowker, 1977.

_____. *Books for the Gifted Child*. New York: Bowker, 1980.

_____. "Book Selection for Young Gifted Readers." *Roeper Review* 3 (1980): 14-17.

_____. "Stimulating Cognitive Growth in Disadvantaged Gifted Children." In *Balancing the Scale for the Disadvantaged Gifted*, edited by Sheri Butterfield. Los Angeles: National/State Leadership Training Institute on the Gifted and the Talented, 1981.

_____. "The Dismal Prospect: The Portrayal of Disability in Basal Readers," *Reading Improvement*, in press.

_____. "Encouraging the Esthetic Impulse in Young Gifted Children," *Roeper Review*, in press.

Austin W. Bunch

Bunch, Austin W. "P.L. 94-142: Will Your School Be Ready?" *Mississippi Educator* 1 (1977): 20.

_____. "What Do We Mean by Learning Disabilities?" *Research in Education* 10, no. 2 (1978): 1-5.

_____. "Racial Differences in Academic Achievement and Learner Self-Concept of School-Labeled EMR Students." *Resource in Education* 11, no. 2 (1979): 82. (Abstracted in Exceptional Child Education Resources 11, no. 2 (1979): 391. ERIC no. 11 2292).

_____. "Non-biased Assessment in Special Education: Some Issues and Possible Answers." *Research in Education* 12, no. 3 (1980): 1-6.

_____. "P.L. 94-142 Impartial Hearings: A Primer." *Research in Education* 12, no. 4 (1980): 1-4.

Dr. Bunch has two articles in progress: "Cautions in the Use of the Bannatyne Recategorization of WISC-R Scores in the Identification of Specific Learning Disabilities" (with Steve F. Chester), and "Regional Compliance with Due Process Rights Under P.L. 94-142: A Statutory View" (with John Winkle).

Ellen C. Fagan

Fagan, Ellen C. *An Evaluation Tool for Rating Performance of Student Teachers in Speech Correction.* Columbia, S.C.: Columbia College, 1979.

_____. "The Speech Therapist: An Identity Crisis in the Public Schools." *Input/Output* 2, no. 1 (1980).

Ms. Fagan has two articles in progress: "Public Law 94-142 and the Speech-Language Pathologist" (with Louise Gervais, Joan Benziewicz, and Connie Cantrell), and "Ellison: A Case Study of the Unisensory Approach" (with Carol Fitzgerald and Kathy Sutton).

Karen H. Harris

Harris, Karen H., and Baskin, Barbara. *The Special Child in the Library.* Chicago: American Library Association, 1976.

_____. *Notes From a Different Drummer: A Guide to Juvenile Fiction Portraying the Handicapped.* New York: Bowker, 1977.

Harris, Karen. "Selecting Library Materials for Exceptional Children." *School Media Quarterly* 8, no. 1 (Fall 1979): 22-28.

Harris, Karen, and Gerber, Paul. "Into the Mainstream: Using Books to Develop Social Skills in Perceptually Impaired Children." *Top of the News* 35, no. 4 (Summer 1979): 379-384.

Harris, Karen. "Selecting Library Materials for Exceptional Children." In *Meeting the Needs of the Handicapped: A Resource for Teachers and Librarians*, eds. Carol H. Thomas and James L. Thomas. Phoenix: Oryx, 1980, pp. 388-97.

Harris, Karen, and Carter, Betty. "Realism in Adolescent Fiction." *Top of the News* 36, no. 3 (Spring 1980): 283-85.

Harris, Karen, and Baskin, Barbara H. "Library Service to the Handicapped Child." *Texas Library Journal* 56, no. 4 (Fall 1980): 193-95.

———. "Book Selection for Young Gifted Readers." *Roeper Review* 3, no. 2 (November-December 1980): 14-17.

———. *Books for the Gifted Child*. New York: Bowker, 1980.

Harris, Karen; Litton, Freddie W.; and Banbury, Mary M. "Materials for Educating Nonhandicapped Students about Their Handicapped Peers," *Teaching Exceptional Children* 13, no. 1 (Fall 1980): 39-43.

———. "The Library Media Specialist as a Mainstreaming Facilitator." *School Media Quarterly* 9, no. 1 (Fall 1980): 40, 49-53.

JoEllen Ostendorf

Ostendorf, JoEllen, and Vaughn, Ester. *Reading Can Be For Everyone . . . A Manual for Public Libraries and Institutions*. Jackson: Mississippi Library Commission, 1979.

Ostendorf, JoEllen; Woodburn, David; Gates, Linda; and McDonald, Hazel. *Criteria for Adequacy of Public Library Service in Mississippi*. Jackson: Mississippi Library Commission, 1979.

Kieth C. Wright

Wright, Kieth C. "Trends in Modern Subject Analysis with Particular Reference to Text Derivative Indexing and Abstracting Methods: The State of the Art." *Information, Part II* 1 (September-October 1972): 1-18.

———. "Social Science Information Characteristics with Particular Reference to the Educational Resources Information Centers (ERIC)." *Journal of the American Society for Information Science* 24 (May-June 1973): 193-204.

———. "Deafness Information Center." *Special Libraries* 66 (February 1975): 74-78.

———. "The Handicapped: Moving From a Curse to a Burden to Citizenship." In *Library Services for the Adult Handicapped: An Institute for Training in Librarianship*, October 9-14, 1977, School of Library and Information Science, State University of New York at Albany. Edited by Lucille Whalen and Joan Miller, and published in *Information: Reports and Bibliographies* 7, no. 2 (1978).

————. *Library and Information Services for the Handicapped*. Littleton, Colo.: Libraries Unlimited, 1978.

————. *Thesaurus-Ethics Index*. Washington, D.C.: Ethics Resource Center, 1981.

Wright, Kieth C.; Harvey, J. P.; and Dickinson, Elizabeth. "Affirmative Action—Handicapped Individuals." In *Affirmative Action and Libraries*. New York: Scarecrow Press, 1981.

————. "Library Education and Handicapped Individuals." *Journal of Education for Librarianship* 21 (Winter 1981): 183-95.

About the Editor

MYRA MACON is an Associate Professor in the Graduate School of Library and Information Science at the University of Mississippi. Her articles have appeared in *Southeastern Librarian, Mississippi Libraries, Top of the News, Arkansas Libraries,* as well as in other journals.